Frances Eales
Steve Oakes

speakout

Upper Intermediate
Workbook with key

PEARSON
Longman

BBC

CONTENTS

CONTENTS

READING

First there was speed dating ... then speed flatmating ... and now ...

SPEED SHRINKING: A THREE-MINUTE CURE?

1 New Yorkers are famous for spending more time with their therapists, or 'shrinks', than with their friends. Whether that's true is open to debate, but with the arrival of speed shrinking, they'll find they have more time left for their personal life, and more cash left in their pockets as well.

2 'You only have three minutes to say your problem <u>and</u> get advice,' said Andu Novac, the first person I spoke to when I arrived at my first speed shrinking event, 'that's so you don't waste time going into detail.'

3 In the newest variant of a format that seems to be inspired by speed dating, participants have the opportunity to seek the advice of eight different therapists, each providing a three-minute session. Speed shrinking is the brainchild of Susan Shapiro, a professor of journalism who has also written a book on the subject. Shapiro stumbled across the idea a few years ago when she herself was looking for a new therapist, and found a way to try out several of them at minimal cost.

4 This evening's event, held in a university lecture hall, is free and has attracted a long queue of people hoping to find a quick cure for their emotional quandaries. Many of those attending are unwilling to talk about their worries to anyone but the therapists, but problems seem to run the gamut from broken relationships, to anxiety about work and money, to general depression as well as a variety of phobias. Advice tends to be succinct and practical, as suits the format.

5 'I'm really unhappy in my job,' Novac tells therapist Adrian Jones. 'I wish I'd become a painter, but now I feel stuck in this position I have at a bank.' 'Follow your dreams,' Jones tells him. 'You may end up poorer but you won't have the regret of not doing what you really want to do.' Jones's advice hardly seems original, but Novac says he is satisfied. 'I liked his style – he seemed to understand, and care,' explains Novac. 'I'm actually looking for a new therapist, and this is a great way to try out eight of them in a short time.'

6 That's actually why many therapists take part in the event, Jones tells us. 'This is a great source of new clients. And it's a good way for me to advertise my new book – I just have it on the table in front of me and refer to it during my sessions.'

7 Some of those seeking advice aren't entirely happy with the format. 'People near me can hear what I'm telling the therapist,' remarks Donna Bersch. 'I feel self-conscious.' But with the loud buzz in the room that sometimes reaches the level of shouting, it's hard to imagine that anyone could actually eavesdrop on another session. Sometimes, they're lucky to be able to hear the person sitting just opposite them!

1A Read the headline and tick the best summary a), b) or c). Then read the article and check.

a) It's about a service where overweight people can lose weight quickly.

b) It's about a service where people can get advice from a therapist in a short time.

c) It's about a service where people get help making their lives simpler.

B Match the people 1–4 with the roles a)–c).

1 Novac *b*   a) therapist
2 Shapiro   b) client
3 Jones   c) founder
4 Bersch

C Are the statements true (T) or false (F)? Underline the words/phrases in the article that helped you.

1 New Yorkers prefer to spend more time with their therapists than with their friends. *F*

2 Shapiro teaches at a university.

3 In speed shrinking, the therapist gets paid cash.

4 A lot of people don't want to tell the reporter what their problems are.

5 Novac thinks that Jones's advice is disappointingly unoriginal.

6 Many of the therapists participate in order to get more business.

7 Bersch doesn't like how noisy it gets sometimes.

8 People sometimes can't hear each other because they talk too softly.

D Write words from the article that match the definitions 1–10.

1 the way that something is organised or designed (paragraph 3) *format*

2 idea or plan that one person has thought of (paragraph 3) _____

3 found by chance (paragraph 3) _____

4 difficult situations where you cannot decide what to do (paragraph 4) _____

5 strong unreasonable fears of particular things (paragraph 4) _____

6 clearly expressed in a few words (paragraph 4) _____

7 a job in a particular organisation (paragraph 5) _____

8 secretly listen to another person's conversation (paragraph 7) _____

GRAMMAR direct and indirect questions

2 Make the therapist's questions with the prompts.

1 Why / you / come / see / me / today?
A: _Why have you come to see me today?_
B: I keep getting headaches.

2 What / these headaches / like?
A: _____
B: Absolutely terrible.

3 What / cause / headaches, / think?
A: _____
B: Mainly thinking about money.

4 What / think / about / moment?
A: _____
B: That clock.

5 that clock / remind / you / anything?
A: _____
B: Yes, money.

6 Why / that?
A: _____
B: Because I'm paying by the minute! Let's stop now.

7 OK. / How / like / pay – / cash / credit card?
A: _____

3A Complete the second sentence so that it has a similar meaning to the first. Use between two and five words, including the word given.

1 Could you introduce us to the director?
WONDER
I _wonder if you could introduce_ us to the director.

2 How much did your camera cost?
CAMERA
Do you mind me _____ cost?

3 What do you do exactly?
TELLING
Would you mind _____ do exactly?

4 Is it really worth upgrading to the new smartphone?
WHETHER
I'd like to know _____ worth upgrading to the new smartphone.

5 Which platform does the Eurostar train leave from?
TRAIN
Can you tell me which platform _____ from?

6 What will he do when he discovers the mistake?
DO
What do you _____ when he discovers the mistake?

B ▶1.1 Listen and check. Then listen and repeat, paying attention to the polite intonation.

VOCABULARY personality

4A Correct the mistake in each phrase.

1 I don't know why you say he's down- ~~on~~ -earth, d _to_

2 I was never particularly about what I eat,

3 Fabio tends to keep in himself and goes to bed very late,

4 My colleague Bill is a real person person

5 He's a good laughter, but with money

a) he tends to be tight-handed and never pays.

b) as he does his best work in the early times, when no one's around.

c) so it's odd that he doesn't really push his weight when we work together.

d) I think he's a real computer gawk, and he's not very practical.

e) but that's changed since I've started getting in cooking.

B Match the sentence halves.

LEARN TO check for accuracy

5A Read the email and use the correction code to correct the mistakes.

Correction code:
v = verb form   gr = grammar   ww = wrong word
sp = spelling   p = punctuation   wo = word order
st = style

To: eduardo132@mymail.com

Hi Eduardo,
Just a quick email to check travel arrangements. Can you let me know exactly when are you arriving ¹___ ?
I've looked on the website and there are three planes from Brazil on Thursday. It's a work day for me, so unfortunately I can't come and meet you at the airport so I attach ²___ a website link to a map of my area. You've already got the adress ³___ I think.
The best thing is to take the RER commuter train to Paris Gare du Nord. It's quickly ⁴___ and not too expensive: ⁵___ From there you can either walk to my apartment or call into the office and I'll give you the key. I'm sure you will require ⁶___ a shower and a rest. Anyway, give me a phone ⁷___ as soon as your plane lands.
See you soon,
Luc

B Correct the mistakes in the email.

C Write a reply email from Eduardo to Luc (120–150 words). Include information about your flight, respond to Eduardo's instructions and ask a question about your stay.

VOCABULARY feelings

1A Put the letters in the correct order to make adjectives. The first letter is underlined.

1 mana<u>g</u>ersribs *embarrassing*

2 hetax<u>e</u>dus _____

3 siftidea<u>s</u> _____

4 herdlil<u>t</u> _____

5 dark<u>a</u>ww _____

6 livedee<u>r</u> _____

7 i<u>a</u>xonus _____

8 gincaf<u>s</u>atin _____

9 grants<u>f</u>ruit _____

10 seedpr<u>i</u>sm _____

B Complete the sentences with the adjectives above.

1 My audition wasn't perfect, but I'm quite _____ with my performance.

2 You look totally _____. Were you working late again last night?

3 I find volcanoes completely _____. I've read every book on the topic.

4 I lost my place in the middle of giving the presentation. It was really _____.

5 We went to Cairo to see the exhibition, but it was closed. It was really _____!

6 My wife came into the shop when I was buying her some perfume. It was quite _____ and I had to hide what I was doing.

7 Seiji had been missing for hours, so his parents were enormously _____ when they found him safe and sound.

8 Jania hasn't phoned for days. I'm getting a bit _____ about whether she's alright.

9 You have a great singing voice. I'm totally _____.

10 I thought I'd failed the exam, so I was absolutely _____ to find out that I'd got top marks.

C Which sentences above contain modifiers (*quite, totally,* etc.) that can be replaced by *very*?

LISTENING

2A ▶ 1.2 Read the advert and listen to the interview. Number the pictures A–C in the order the dreams are mentioned.

A   B   C

_____ _____ _____

★★ DREAMSRREAL.COM ★★

Do you have experiences you've always wanted to try but never thought were possible?

Whether your dream is ordinary or extraordinary, it's special to us! With DreamsRreal.com, there's always a first time – we guarantee it!

B Listen again and choose the correct answer.

1 What did the first client want?

 a) to appear with a rock star in a live concert

 b) people to recognise her talent

 c) to play in front of a large number of people

2 Why does Owen Winters find his job at DreamsRreal.com easy?

 a) It's similar to his previous job.

 b) He has worked in business for many years.

 c) He knows a lot of people in the music business.

3 What is the secret about the supersonic flight?

 a) the name of the client who wants to fly

 b) the financial details of the flight

 c) where the plane comes from

4 How did the person with Tom Cruise make-up feel about the experience?

 a) He loved all the attention.

 b) He didn't enjoy it.

 c) He didn't like the bodyguards.

5 What happened to the woman who wanted to go into space?

 a) She couldn't afford it at first but now she can.

 b) She was originally disappointed but now she's going to achieve her dream.

 c) It has taken DreamsRreal.com a long time to plan and organise the trip.

C Listen again. How many of the clients' dreams are connected with pop culture (P), transport (T) or history (H)?

GRAMMAR present perfect and past simple

3 Complete the sentences with the present perfect or past simple form of the verbs in brackets.

1 Is there something you _have always wanted_ (always want) to do but somehow _____ (never manage) to?

2 Not long ago our company _____ (have) a client who _____ (want) to be a rock star.

3 I _____ (work) as a production manager in the film business for many years, till just a few years ago.

4 How much _____ (the concert / cost) last year, and _____ the cost _____ (go) up since then?

5 What other dreams _____ you _____ (make) come true recently?

6 We _____ (just finish) working with a client who wants to fly across the Atlantic Ocean on a supersonic aeroplane.

7 One client wanted to fly in space but that wasn't possible back when she first _____ (request) it.

8 Since then it _____ (become) possible for ordinary people to go into space.

4 Complete the conversations with the present perfect or past simple form of the verbs in the box.

speak	forget	leave	happen	not ask
be (x2)	get back	see	have (x2)	stay	go

1 **A:** _____ anyone _____ my pen?

  B: What does it look like?

  A: It's silver. I'm sure I _____ it on the table before we _____ to lunch.

2 **A:** _____ you _____ to Kiera today?

  B: No, and I _____ her yet if she wants to come out with us tomorrow.

3 **A:** Hi, Suzie. When _____ you _____ from holiday?

  B: A few days ago but I _____ (already) it. There _____ over 300 emails in my inbox!

  A: I sympathise! The same thing _____ after my break.

4 **A:** Do you know anyone who _____ bird flu?

  B: No, thankfully. What about you?

  A: Frank _____ away from school last week as one of the other kids _____ a bad fever, but it was a false alarm.

  B: Yes, so far everyone in the family _____ OK.

VOCABULARY PLUS word formation

5A Complete the quotes with the noun form of the words in capitals.

1	As far as playing jazz, no other art form, other than conversation, can give the _____ of spontaneous interaction. *Stan Getz, musician*	SATISFYING
2	_____ is giving more than you can, and pride is taking less than you need. *Kahlil Gibran, writer*	GENEROUS
3	There is no such thing as pure pleasure; some _____ always goes with it. *Ovid, poet*	ANXIOUS
4	Most things in life are moments of pleasure and a lifetime of _____; photography is a moment of _____ and a lifetime of pleasure. *Tony Benn, politician*	EMBARRASSED
5	There can be no deep _____ where there is not deep love. *Martin Luther King Jr, civil rights activist*	DISAPPOINTING
6	If I ever completely lost my _____ I would be frightened half to death. *Paul Lynde, actor*	NERVOUS
7	The universe may have a purpose, but nothing we know suggests that, if so, this purpose has any _____ to ours. *Bertrand Russell, philosopher*	SIMILAR
8	Men lose more conquests by their own _____ than by any virtue in the woman. *Ninon de L'Enclos, writer*	AWKWARD
9	A life of _____ is inevitable for any coach whose main enjoyment is winning. *Chuck Noll, American football coach*	FRUSTRATED

B Which of the quotes are about music (M), sport (S), or another topic (A)?

C Tick the quotations you agree with and put a cross next to those you don't agree with.

CIRCUIT TRAINING

Limited [1]_____ – only two places left!

[2]_____ up now.

Fill [3]_____ your personal details on this form and pay the deposit today!

(deposit is non-[4]_____)

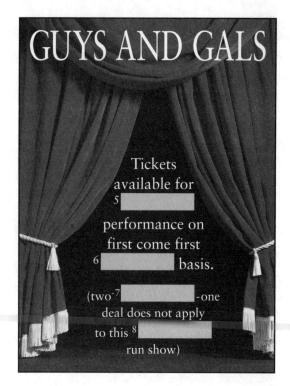

GUYS AND GALS

Tickets available for [5]_____ performance on first come first [6]_____ basis.

(two-[7]_____-one deal does not apply to this [8]_____ run show)

VOCABULARY adverts

1 Complete the adverts above with the words in the box.

limited	refundable	served	for	in
sign	enrolment	matinée		

FUNCTION polite enquiries

2 Correct two mistakes in each underlined phrase in the conversation.

A: Eden Gardens Hotel. How can I help you?

B: Hi, [1]<u>I'm call to enquiry about</u> a reservation I made. The booking reference is 6714.

A: OK. How can I help you?

B: I need to change the dates to one week later. [2]<u>I was wandering is that</u> possible, and how much the change will cost.

A: Ah, it's a two-for-one weekend deal.

B: Yes. [3]<u>Would there be any chances of get</u> the same price for the following weekend?

A: I'm not sure.

B: [4]<u>I'd appreciated it whether you could</u> make an exception.

A: I need to ask my supervisor.

B: OK ...

A: No, sorry, we can't do that.

B: [5]<u>Would your mind saying me</u> why it's so complicated to change?

A: Sorry, it's policy. Online special deals are non-refundable, non-transferable.

B: [6]<u>Do you me mind asking what is your name</u> ?

A: We aren't allowed to give our full names.

B: In that case, [7]<u>I like to speak about</u> your supervisor.

3 ▶ 1.3 Listen to the intonation of the enquiries. Write polite (P) or impolite (I).

1a) _P_ b) ___   5a) ___ b) ___
2a) ___ b) ___   6a) ___ b) ___
3a) ___ b) ___   7a) ___ b) ___
4a) ___ b) ___

LEARN TO manage enquiries

4A Put the words in the correct order to make sentences.

1 your / I'd / appreciate / help / really
I'd really appreciate your help.

2 that / just / difficult / it's / be / sorry / to ...

_____

3 a / me / with / minute / bear

_____

4 question / keeping / got / you / I've / one / if / I'm / more / not

_____

5 you / keep / to / sorry

_____

6 hold / minute / just / you / a / I'll / can / on / see?

_____

B ▶ 1.4 Listen to the conversation or read the audio script on page 74 and number the phrases above in the correct order. Two of them are not used.

GRAMMAR present perfect simple and continuous

1A Match the sentence pairs.

1 She's done
   She's been doing
   a) her homework since she got home from school.
   b) all her homework.

2 I've sent
   I've been sending
   a) twenty-five application letters this morning.
   b) application letters all morning. I need a break!

3 Pete's called
   Pete's been calling
   a) you all evening. Is your mobile on?
   b) and left you a message.

4 I've read this magazine.
   I've been reading this magazine.
   a) Do you want to borrow it when I've finished?
   b) Do you want to borrow it?

5 Julia's gone to the gym –
   Julia's been going to the gym,
   a) and she's ten kilos lighter now.
   b) shall I ask her to call you back?

6 The temperature has dropped
   The temperature has been dropping
   a) all day
   b) to minus thirty.

B ▶ 2.1 Listen to the sentences and repeat what you hear. Pay attention to the stress and rhythm.

2 Complete the blog entry with the present perfect simple or continuous form of the verbs in brackets. If both are possible, use the continuous form.

I ¹_____ (travel) all my life and I ²_____ (visit) more than twenty-five countries, many of them less rich than my own. I ³_____ (often / want) to take something to repay people for their hospitality but I ⁴_____ (never / know) what to choose. Anyway, recently I ⁵_____ (explore) a number of websites that give advice and I ⁶_____ (find) a great one called stuffyourrucksack.com. It was created by Kate Humble, who ⁷_____ (present) wildlife programmes on television for many years. It's a beautifully simple idea: the website matches up charities that need stuff with people who are willing to provide and deliver it. Travellers ⁸_____ (tell) the website about 187 organisations in 81 countries, and these include schools needing books or footballs, orphanages needing clothes and toys and trade organisations needing mobiles. So far it looks as if the response ⁹_____ (be) good and the website ¹⁰_____ (recently / appear) in a 'Find of the Year' survey of new sites.

VOCABULARY social issues

3A Write the problem next to each headline. The first letters are given.

OIL POURS INTO OCEAN FROM DAMAGED TANKER
1 po_____

Thousands rely on aid centres for food as crops fail
2 fa_____

NUMBER OF PEOPLE SLEEPING ON CITY STREETS RISING
3 ho_____

DOCTORS' FEARS ABOUT OVERWEIGHT SIX-YEAR-OLDS
4 ob_____

COCAINE USE ON THE RISE
5 dr_____ ab_____

CHEAP ALCOHOL FUELS PROBLEMS IN TOWN CENTRES
6 dr_____

Fewer marriages last a lifetime
7 di_____

SOUTH SEES FOURTH MONTH WITH NO RAIN
8 dr_____

THOUSANDS OVERSPEND ON CREDIT CARDS
9 de_____

CENTRE OPENS FOR WOMEN ATTACKED AT HOME
10 do_____ vi_____

HALF OF PENSIONERS CAN'T AFFORD TO HEAT HOMES
11 po_____

VILLAGERS WALK 20 KMS TO FETCH WATER
12 la_____ of dr_____ wa_____

B ▶ 2.2 Listen and check.

C Listen again and write the words/phrases next to the correct stress pattern.

O	1_____	2_____
Oo	3_____	
oO	4_____	
Ooo	5_____	6_____
	7_____	
oOo	8_____	
oOoo	9_____	
o oO	10_____	
oOo Ooo	11_____	
o o Oo Oo	12_____	

LISTENING

4A Read the text and answer the questions.

1 What is the aim of the organisation? How does it want to achieve it?

_____

2 Which ideas 1–8 are connected to the environment (E) and which are connected to personal and social development (PS)?

In 2004, a small London-based community organisation called **We Are What We Do** published a book, **Change the world for a fiver** *. It contained fifty simple actions which ordinary people could do to make the world a better place. Now it is a global movement with a lively website, millions of active participants, and more than 130 ideas for actions.

Its motto is:

SMALL ACTIONS × LOTS OF PEOPLE = BIG CHANGE.

Ideas include:

1 Use a biro from start to finish **E**

2 Smile and smile back ___

3 Do something you think you are unable to do ___

4 Buy fairly traded products ___

5 Remember people's names ___

6 Turn off the tap when you brush your teeth ___

7 Say 'no' to plastic bags wherever possible ___

8 Learn one good joke ___

*£5

B ⏵2.3 Listen to four people speaking about their experiences. Which ideas 1–8 above did each one try?

1 ___   2 ___   3 ___   4 ___ ___

C Listen again and make notes about:

a) why the speaker chose that particular action.

b) what problems each speaker experienced.

Speaker 1 a) _____
　　　　　 b) _____

Speaker 2 a) _____
　　　　　 b) _____

Speaker 3 a) _____
　　　　　 b) _____

Speaker 4 a) _____
　　　　　 b) _____

VOCABULARY *PLUS* verbs/nouns with the same form

5A Complete the sentences with the correct form of the words in the box.

increase	decrease	produce	import
export	present	project	sponsor
record	permit	appeal	suspect

1 In the 2008 Olympics, Usain Bolt set three world _____ including the 100 metres.

2 Children's phone ownership has _____ dramatically to an all-time high.

3 Germany _____ more items to other countries than any other country in the world.

4 If you stay in Spain for more than ninety days you need to apply for a resident's _____.

5 CCTV cameras have been successful, with a huge _____ in incidents of violence.

6 Police have launched a nationwide _____ for help to find a missing sixteen-year-old.

7 The BBC _____ a number of different charities including Comic Relief and SportsAid.

8 Ladies and Gentlemen, I'd like to _____ our speaker for tonight, the well-known scientist, Rajesh Gokhale.

9 Last year the farm _____ twenty tonnes of apples and sent them direct to supermarkets.

10 The National Gallery is planning to _____ gigantic images of Picasso paintings onto the outside of the building.

11 The USA _____ more coffee from coffee-producing countries than any other country.

12 The police have arrested the chief _____ in connection with the bank robbery.

B Underline the stress in the words you wrote in 1–12 above.

records

READING

1A You are going to read about a course that trains people to be spies. Read the list and tick the three things that you think are most important for a spy to be able to do.

break into a property

drive fast without getting into an accident

follow someone without getting caught

pretend they are someone else

use karate or other martial arts

win the trust of a stranger

B Read the article. Which three things from the list above are mentioned?

1 _____   2 _____   3 _____

SO YOU WANT TO BE A **SPY**?

1 Despite recent developments in surveillance technology, a camera is no substitute for the human eye, and there will always be a need for that most secretive of professions, the spy. In the BBC 3 series, *Spy*, a group of eight volunteers took a two-month crash course in spying. Their trainers were former spies and experts in fields such as psychology and body language.

2 Before they joined the course, the would-be spies were allowed to tell only one person what they were really doing; for everyone else, they had to invent a believable cover story to explain their two-month absence. A couple of them immediately got into trouble when their story of a two-month job in New York resulted in friends promising to visit them.

3 As soon as they arrived at headquarters and before they had time to unpack, the eight 'spies' faced their first challenge: they had just ten minutes to talk their way into the flat of a complete stranger and be seen by their trainers drinking a glass of water on the balcony. It's a great task, and one often used by real spy agencies to test their spies' abilities to act under pressure and think up plausible reasons to gain access to places.

4 The recruits learnt about surveillance techniques including how to 'go grey' and disappear into a crowd and also how to organise a surveillance operation on a house. This meant breaking into the property, planting secret cameras and bugs, and fixing tracking devices to cars.

5 Another week, the recruits had to go undercover, adopt new identities and take temporary jobs in a gym, a clothes shop and a barber's. They had to convince their co-workers that they were genuine, gain their trust and finally persuade one of them to do something wrong, for example to lie or to sign a false document.

6 At the end of the experience, what qualities did they think were important for being a spy? 'A spy needs to be a quick thinker, work well under pressure and be able to blend in.' It helps to be a woman: 'Sandy our female trainer loved to remind us how women made better spies.' So if you are a tall male it's probably not worth applying. And were any of the participants keen to become a spy? Certainly not one married candidate: 'A Service insider told me that there is an exceptionally high divorce rate in the spy business with a lot of agents marrying their secretaries – the only person they can confide in and trust.' Perhaps that's why James Bond spent most of his life single.

C Match the quotes a)–e) with one of the paragraphs in the article.

a) I had to get right underneath and it was difficult to fix it on securely. ____

b) I'm a location manager for a TV company and we need a place to film. ____

c) I'm going on safari and I'll be back in two months. ____

d) It's just another thing that girls do better than boys! ____

e) I used to work at a men's clothing store in Soho – that's how I got this job. ____

D Write words and phrases from the article that match the definitions 1–8.

1 can't replace (paragraph 1) *is no substitute for*

2 fast and intensive period of training (paragraph 1) _____

3 someone who wants to be something; potential (paragraph 2) _____

4 believable (paragraph 3) _____

5 become unnoticeable (paragraph 4) _____

6 work secretly with a different identity (paragraph 5) _____

7 look similar to everything around you (paragraph 6) _____

8 tell secrets to (paragraph 6) _____

VOCABULARY surveillance

2 Complete the sentences. The first letters are given.

1 A sp_____ camera in the road measures how fast you drive.

2 If you are ac_____ for something, you are responsible for it.

3 If something is a de_____ to crime, it acts to stop it.

4 When people break into your private life, it's an in_____ of privacy.

5 A person who always obeys the law is a la_____ citizen.

6 One system for identifying a car is number plate re_____.

7 To lo_____ is to make a systematic official record of events.

8 Carefully watch something over a period of time, for example a nurse mo_____ a patient's condition.

9 An extremely small electronic object used in computers is a mi_____ .

10 If you ke____ tr____ of someone who is moving, you always know their position.

GRAMMAR the passive

3A Complete the sentences with the passive form of the verbs in brackets.

STRANGE BUT TRUE!

1 All gondolas in Venice, Italy, must _____ (paint) black, except if they belong to a high official.

2 The modern Frisbee_____ (invent) by the Frisbie Pie Company in 1946 when their pie tins _____ (throw) around by employees during breaks.

3 Over the centuries, Korea _____ (invade) more times than any other country in the world.

4 The white surface of the Taj Mahal _____ (gradually / damage) by pollution and is turning yellow.

5 British guidebooks in the nineteenth century advised women to put pins in their mouths to avoid _____ (kiss) in the dark when trains went through tunnels.

6 You are more likely_____ (kill) by a champagne cork than a poisonous spider, but most people are more afraid of spiders.

7 Kangaroos can_____ (find) in the wild in only two countries: Australia and New Zealand.

8 When Christopher Columbus 'discovered' America in 1492, the continent _____ (already / explore) by the Vikings from Norway over three centuries earlier.

B Two of the facts above are false. Which are they?

4 Complete the sentences with the correct active or passive form of the verbs in brackets.

TECHNOLOGY UPDATE

Currently hundreds of trainee medical students [1]_____ (teach) through the online virtual world *Second Life*. Once a day students [2]_____ (send) to locations in the online world to treat computer-generated patients. When they are there, virtual equipment can [3]_____ (use) to check the patients at the scene and then the trainees can [4]_____ (decide) the best course of action. The training tool has been a great success so far and from next year it [5]_____ (use) at a number of medical schools around the world.

Pollution is an ever-growing problem in our cities but in the near future a new system [6]_____ (allow) traffic managers to identify pollution hotspots. The movement of cars through the city will be able to [7]_____ (alter) by changing the traffic light sequencing to direct cars away from problem areas. A computer [8]_____ (also / send) commuters warning text alerts on their mobile phones so they can decide how to avoid the hotspot. The new pollution monitoring system [9]_____ (test) successfully for the first time at a trial last month and could [10]_____ (introduce) as soon as next year.

LEARN TO use formal written language

5A Correct the mistakes in the underlined phrases.

Dear Sir or Madam,

[1]<u>I am writing with regard for</u> my stay in one of your hotels.

I stayed at the Riley Hotel in Belfast from June 14 to 16 and experienced a number of problems. Firstly, the room had not been properly cleaned. Secondly, there were no tea- or coffee-making facilities in the room. Finally, there was a party in the room under mine and it kept me awake until early morning.

[2]<u>I have already persuaded this matter</u> with the hotel manager but she was quite rude and suggested that I write to you. [3]<u>In order to dissolve this matter</u> I am requesting that you refund the money for my stay at the hotel. [4]<u>Please contract me within ten days</u> of the date of this letter [5]<u>to convince that this step has been taken.</u>

[6]<u>Thank you for your promptly attention to this matter.</u>

[7]<u>Yours faithlessly,</u>

Viola Gresham

[8]<u>CC: hotel receipt</u>

B Write a letter of complaint (120–150 words) to a restaurant where you recently had an important lunch, e.g., a meeting or a first date. Include three things that went wrong.

FUNCTION opinions

1A Cross out the unnecessary words in the numbered sentences.

A: Do you think students should be allowed to use their phones in class?

B: Yeah, [1]I'm not in favour of that. [2]The way what I see it is that students would be more motivated if they could use phones, maybe to make short movies or things like that.

A: OK, [3]you've got a the point there, but you know how kids are. [4]It seems that to me that they'd just start texting each other whenever they were bored.

B: [5]I'm agree to some extent. They would certainly need very strict rules, you know, about turning them on and off. But phones could be useful for things like practising languages or setting homework reminders.

A: Yes, [6]I can suppose so, but what about bullying, you know, kids sending each other nasty messages? Or phones could be a target for thieves.

B: [7]Is fair enough but either of those things could happen after school.

A: Hmm. [8]I see your point is, but [9]I'm still not being convinced. I think on balance it's better to keep them out of classes.

B: [10]I don't disagree. I think we should encourage them.

B ▶2.4 **Listen or read the audio script on page 75 to check.**

C ▶2.5 **Listen to the opinion phrases and repeat what you hear.**

But you said no mobile phones in class

LEARN TO support your viewpoint

2 Complete the second sentence so that it has a similar meaning to the first. Start with the words given.

1 Latest research has found that profiles on social networking sites are accurate descriptions of people's personalities.

According _____.

2 Kids still enjoy dolls, electric train sets and Lego.

Toys like _____

3 Japan is one of many countries where fish is an important part of the diet.

In many countries, for instance _____

4 People are said to be attracted to partners who look like them.

Apparently, people _____

5 The experiment shows coffee's ability to increase short-term memory.

It's been shown _____

6 Media Studies, Sports Studies and Dance are examples of 'soft' subjects and are no longer being offered in some colleges.

'Soft' subjects such _____

7 For example, there was a situation where twins separated at birth lived identical lives.

Take the case _____

8 Everyone knows that children under five who watch too much television lack basic communication skills.

It's a well-known _____

VOCABULARY opinion adjectives

3A Put the letters in bold in the correct order to make adjectives. The first letter is underlined.

A: What are the drink drive laws in your country?

B: Zero tolerance. It's [1]**glelial** _____to drive if you've drunk any alcohol at all.

A: That seems like a [2]**beenliss** _____ law to me.

A: Models shouldn't wear fur. It's [3]**chutainel** _____ to kill animals just for fashion.

B: I'd go along with you there, but what about in really cold places?

A: Well obviously it's [4]**fuijablesti** _____ then, but I'm talking about fashion.

A: I think it's [5]**liveinbeta** _____ that one day everyone will have a microchip under their skin from birth.

B: Really? I find the whole idea deeply [6]**birdugsint** _____.

A: Jan's gone too far this time! His idea at the meeting was [7]**uregasouto** _____!

B: Do you think so? I thought it was silly but fairly [8]**finevosfine** _____.

A: I don't agree.

B ▶2.6 **Listen and write the adjectives next to the correct stress patterns. Then listen again and repeat what you hear.**

Ooo   [1]_____
oOo   [2]_____ [3]_____ [4]_____
ooOo   [5]_____
oOoo   [6]_____
oOooo [7]_____
ooOoo [8]_____

GRAMMAR verb tense review

1 Complete the article with the past simple, present perfect simple or present perfect continuous forms of the verbs in brackets.

Grandmother passes driving test on 950th attempt

Cha Sa-soon [1]_____ (want) to drive for years, and last week she [2]_____ (move) a step closer to that dream: she [3]_____ (pass) the written exam for a driving licence on her 950th attempt.

'I [4]_____ (try) to pass this test for over four years,' said the sixty-eight-year-old grandmother, 'And now I [5]_____ (finally do) it. Over the past two years a lot of people [6]_____ (tell) me I'm crazy, but I don't mind. If you have a dream, you can't give up.'

She [7]_____ (become) a bit of a legend at the testing centre. 'It [8]_____ (be) difficult to see her fail so many times,' said the centre director. 'And we [9]_____ (hope) that sooner or later she would get through. She'll be missed, that's for sure,' he [10]_____ (add). 'A day without Cha is like a day without our favourite granny.'

Mrs Sa-soon [11]_____ (spend) over five million Korean won on fees so far; now she just needs to pass the practical test, and after she [12]_____ (pass) that she'll be given a licence.

2 Match the sentence pairs.

1   I've never seen snow   a) until I went to Austria.
    I never saw snow   b) in my life.

2   I couldn't find a job   a) after university.
    I haven't been able to   b) since university.
    find a job

3   No one has seen her   a) a week ago.
    She was last seen   b) in the past week.

4   I've been seeing a therapist   a) three times now.
    I've seen a therapist   b) regularly.

5   Many students have   a) recently.
    been arriving late   b) the other day.
    Many students arrived late

6   I thought I understood this   a) so far.
    I've understood everything   b) before now.

VOCABULARY review

3 Complete the sentences with the correct word/phrase.

1   pulls her weight / is particular
    a) Lena's a good worker: she _____ around the office.
    b) Tessa _____ about leaving her desk tidy at the end of the day.

2   awkward / embarrassed
    a) The article is called 'Top health questions you are too _____ to ask'.
    b) I was with my husband when we ran into his ex-wife. It was very _____.

3   relieved / satisfied
    a) Beth thought she'd lost her passport so she was incredibly _____ to find it.
    b) The boss seemed _____ with my work on the report and he's giving me tomorrow off.

4   non-refundable / two-for-one
    a) The _____ deal is only available on Monday evenings.
    b) A _____ deposit is required when booking the holiday.

5   monitor / keep track of
    a) When I'm working on a painting I never _____ the time. It drives my wife crazy.
    b) We're going to try you on this new treatment and we'll _____ your progress carefully.

6   invasion / deterrent
    a) Are the fines working as a/an _____ to pollution?
    b) Are full body scanners at airports a/an _____ of privacy?

7   illegal / unethical
    a) Hunting elephants is _____ but hunting deer is allowed, with a permit.
    b) Buying an essay from the internet and saying you wrote it is totally _____.

8   disturbing / outrageous
    a) It was absolutely _____ that the workers were told of their job losses by text message.
    b) I found the programme about child beauty competitions slightly _____.

9   justifiable / sensible
    a) How _____ is it to buy medicine over the internet from someone you don't know?
    b) Is it ever _____ to kill someone?

4A Look at the underlined sounds in each group. Circle the word with the different sound.

1 dr<u>ou</u>ght, exh<u>au</u>sted, <u>aw</u>kward

2 v<u>i</u>olence, fam<u>i</u>ne, exc<u>i</u>ted

3 ob<u>e</u>sity, inv<u>a</u>sion, matin<u>ée</u>

4 <u>i</u>llegal, sens<u>i</u>ble, m<u>i</u>crochip

5 non-ref<u>u</u>ndable, drug ab<u>u</u>se, j<u>u</u>stifiable

B ▶ RC1.1 Listen and check. Then listen and repeat.

5 Complete the articles with the active or passive form of the verbs.

Improve your IQ

In a recent experiment, two groups of people [1]_____ to spend time writing down some sentences, one group about a typical university professor and the other about a football hooligan. They then [2]_____ a trivia test. The result: the 'professor' group [3]_____ much higher than the other group. It [4]_____ that this is due to 'priming' the brain in a positive way to get it to think more intelligently.

> think
> score
> complete
> ask

Together forever?

In an experiment which is being carried out in the USA, married couples [5]_____ having a conversation. They [6]_____ to discuss topics that [7]_____ some friction in their relationship in the past. Based on just several minutes of the material, it can [8]_____ with high accuracy who will still be together in fifteen years, and who will divorce.

> cause
> film
> predict
> ask

Care bears for the elderly?

In the coming years, many countries [9]_____ the challenge of an aging population and a shortage of nurses. The Japanese-produced Robo-bear [10]_____ to help with tasks such as lifting and moving patients. The first human-shaped robots [11]_____ to be too frightening for patients and so now the Robo-bear [12]_____ the head of a friendly cartoon bear.

> find
> give
> face
> design

6 Read the clues and complete the crossword with social issues.

Across

3 This causes damage to the environment.

4 When people are very poor.

5 When you cannot afford to pay your bills.

6 When a husband and wife separate legally.

7 This is a health problem. People are becoming fatter.

8 When people drink too much alcohol.

9 When people suffer illness and death because there is no food.

Down

1 When people have nowhere to live.

2 If a husband beats his wife, this is _____. (2 words)

8 If you take illegal substances, this is _____ abuse.

7 Put the words in the correct order.

1 your / I / but / point / take

_____

2 of / in / that / favour / I'm

_____

3 with / don't / you / agree / I

_____

4 extent / some / to / but / agree / I

_____

5 not / still / I'm / convinced

_____

6 've / but / there / a / You / point / got

_____

7 what / mean / I / but / know / you

_____

8 not / sure / so / I'm

_____

VOCABULARY *PLUS* word formation

8 Find and correct the mistakes in the formation of the words in bold.

| Friends |
| News |
| Search |
| Games |

THE WORST DAY OF MY LIFE

My first solo piano concert in the music academy – it should have been the best day of my life. Of course, I felt a touch of ¹**anxious** before the performance and I arrived early only to find that they had replaced the piano that I had practised on with a different one. The new piano wasn't bad, but because of my ²**nervous** and ³**frustrating** I made a lot of mistakes. I was very ⁴**disappointment** in myself and it was all very ⁵**embarrassment**. Afterwards there was a lot of ⁶**awkward** at the reception, since people didn't know what to say, and the whole experience was so ⁷**exhaustion** that I just wanted to sleep. In the end I had one ⁸**satisfaction** moment, when a famous concert pianist came up to me and told me that he had had a ⁹**similarity** experience early in his career, and offered me the chance to play in another concert. It was only his ¹⁰**generous** that gave me a second chance and stopped me from giving up there and then!

1_____	6_____
2_____	7_____
3_____	8_____
4_____	9_____
5_____	10_____

GRAMMAR direct and indirect questions

9 Change the direct questions into indirect questions.

1 What were you like ten years ago?
   Can you tell _____?

2 How do you think you've changed?
   I'd be interested _____.

3 What have you done that you are most proud of?
   Would you mind telling _____?

4 Is it possible for a person to stay the same all his life?
   I wonder _____.

5 Who has influenced you the most?
   Could you tell _____?

6 Would you like to direct a movie yourself?
   I was wondering _____.

FUNCTION making polite enquiries

10A Underline the correct alternative(s).

1 Yes, Mr Lawson. How can I *help/refund/answer* you?

2 *I was wondering/would wonder/wonder* whether I could move it to the week after.

3 And would there be any chance of *book/booking/to book* in a friend?

4 *Could you/Would you mind/I'd appreciate* telling me if that's going to cost more?

5 *Can you/Could you/Do you* tell me why I've been kept on hold for so long? It's really annoying.

6 I'd *appreciate it/thank you/be grateful* if you could put it in an email.

B Match replies a)–f) to enquiries 1–6 above.

a) The computers are extremely slow today, I'm very sorry. ___

b) Just a moment. Sorry, you've just taken the last place. ___

c) Of course. I'll confirm all the details straightaway. ___

d) Sorry to keep you. That will be 250 euros extra. ___

e) I'm calling to enquire about a booking I made last week. ___

f) Bear with me a minute. Yes, that booking is transferable. ___

VOCABULARY *PLUS* verbs/nouns with the same form

11A Complete the news report with the correct form of the words in the box.

| decrease | record | increase | research | desert |
| sponsor | project | appeal | import | permit |

A group of rock stars are ¹_____ for ²_____ to fund a new ³_____ aimed at preventing malaria. Recent medical ⁴_____ shows there is a dramatic ⁵_____ in the disease when malaria nets are provided for families.

Fifty-two tourists have been rescued from the ⁶_____ near the Step Pyramid in Egypt after temperatures reached 49 degrees Celsius – the highest level ever ⁷_____ in the area. The tourists were stranded when their bus broke down. The group's tour operator has been arrested for failing to obtain a ⁸_____ to conduct business in the area.

And in business, a number of European countries are planning to cut ⁹_____ from the United States as trade tensions continue. The USA has recently ¹⁰_____ taxes on all goods coming from abroad to an all-time high.

B ▶ RC1.2 Listen or read the audio script on page 75 to check.

C Underline the stress in words 1–10. Then listen again and check.

TEST

Circle the correct option to complete the sentences.

1 Do you know _____?
a) she's going   b) whether she's going
c) where is she going

2 The show is only on a _____, so let's see it as soon as possible.
a) limited run   b) limited enrolment
c) first come first served

3 A: Your clothes are soaking wet!
B: Yes, I _____ in the rain.
a) walked   b) 've walked   c) 've been walking

4 Domestic _____ is a growing problem in times of unemployment.
a) violence   b) divorce   c) drunkenness

5 They _____ the report for days and it's still not finished.
a) 've been writing   b) 've written
c) 've been written

6 Could you tell me _____?
a) what means that   b) what that means
c) what does that mean

7 I'm phoning _____ a course.
a) to enquire about   b) about enquiring
c) enquire about

8 Corruption isn't only deeply _____, it's also _____.
a) disturbing/inoffensive   b) justifiable/unethical
c) disturbing/unethical

9 We need to _____ all their comings and goings over the next twenty-four hours.
a) log   b) keep track   c) permit

10 I felt some _____ when I couldn't make myself understood in Spanish.
a) frustrating   b) frustration   c) frustrated

11 Teachers want _____ what students don't like.
a) to tell   b) to be told   c) being told

12 A: What is the _____ between a clock, a coin and a mountain?
B: They all have faces.
a) similar   b) similarness   c) similarity

13 I _____ Rita lately. Is she OK?
a) didn't see   b) haven't yet seen   c) haven't seen

14 A: What _____?
B: She's great! I really like her.
a) 's your new boss like   b) does your new boss like
c) 's like your new boss

15 My mum was _____ thrilled to hear the news.
a) very   b) fairly   c) absolutely

16 I _____ ten cups of coffee and it's only noon.
a) had   b) 've had   c) 've been having

17 A: They really shouldn't have closed the school.
B: I agree _____, but there were good reasons for it.
a) for some extent   b) to some extent
c) to some point

18 The president's _____ for the early release of the hostages has not been successful.
a) sponsor   b) appeal   c) present

19 Some say that a guard dog is the best _____ to crime.
a) deterrent   b) monitor   c) surveillance

20 We've been very lucky _____.
a) yet   b) already   c) so far

21 They found out that all their movements _____ by CCTV cameras.
a) were being monitored   b) were monitoring
c) have monitored

22 Would there be _____ holding my place?
a) any chance for   b) any chance of
c) any chance

23 She's been feeling a lot of _____ about the new job – that's why she can't sleep.
a) generosity   b) anxiety   c) satisfaction

24 _____, the minimum voting age should be sixteen.
a) The way I see it   b) I'm against
c) It seems to me as

25 The most _____ way forward seems to be to organise a meeting to discuss the issue calmly.
a) sensible   b) inevitable   c) outrageous

26 The murderer _____ yet.
a) hasn't caught   b) wasn't caught
c) hasn't been caught

27 They are shipping in food, but thousands will still die of hunger in the _____.
a) obesity   b) debt   c) famine

28 He never pays for anything, he's so _____.
a) tight-fisted   b) generous   c) down to earth

29 You got the highest mark in the exam? I'm really _____.
a) exhausted   b) anxious   c) impressed

30 He _____ once last week.
a) hasn't visited   b) didn't visit   c) has visited

TEST RESULT | /30

LISTENING

1A Read about the signs of addiction to social networking. Which ones are physical symptoms?

Are you addicted to social networking?

The signs:

- forgetting to eat
- ignoring friends and family
- anxiety
- lying to spend time doing it
- very bad headaches
- always thinking about doing it
- sleep problems
- problems with school or work
- dry or aching eyes
- not taking proper breaks

B ▶ 3.1 Listen to five people talking about their addictions. Write the number of the speaker (1–5) next to the signs in Exercise 1A. There may be more than one possibility.

C Listen again. Make two changes to each of the sentences (1–5) so they match what you hear.

1 I actually found it quite strange talking to their face because I'm much more used to interacting with people online.

2 It's the quizzes and other applications that interest me, like there's always a new quiz or test for something.

3 I would often miss lunch so I could continue chatting.

4 To be fair, she probably asked me direct first but I suppose I'd got so involved in the site that I didn't hear her.

5 When a chat message arrived, I couldn't resist, I'd stop what I was doing and join the chat.

VOCABULARY behaviour

2A Put the letters in the correct order to make adjectives. The first letter is underlined.

1	g̲te no twih	_get on with_	6	nompmile̲ct _____
2	i̲rceisitc	_____	7	ak̲te crea _____
3	u̲pt ffo	_____	8	vieg ni _____
4	p̲ya ntintotea ot	_____	9	goren̲i _____
5	bobtnur̲s	_____	10	n̲cegetl _____

B Complete the text with the correct form of the words above.

My childhood was fairly happy. My mother worked full-time as a hairdresser but she still [1]_____ of us very well, cooking for us and taking an interest in our schoolwork. When I look back now, however, I realise that she often [2]_____ her own health to look after us. I wasn't close to my father. He'd say 'Hi' at breakfast from behind his newspaper, then he [3]_____ us. This suited us fine and we used to play outside all day. We never [4]_____ the time and often were late for dinner.

My brother, Ethan, and I were exact opposites. When we had homework, I tended to [5]_____ (it) and often didn't even finish it, while he just [6]_____ it and always got good marks. As a result, in the end-of-term reports, teachers always [7]_____ him on his hard work and [8]_____ me for being lazy. In arguments, my brother was always the [9]_____ one and would never change his mind; he called me a softy because I always [10]_____ so easily.

GRAMMAR used to, would, be/get used to

3 Underline the correct alternative.

1 I'm *not/not getting* used to having so many people around – I *used to be/'m used to being* alone.

2 I *used to/would* think I was right about everything, so I'm not *used to/getting used to* being wrong.

3 I can't *be used to/get used to* the local accent, so I think my English is worse than it *used to/would* be.

4 My friends and I would *take/taking* long walks, and we used to *stay/staying* out late every night.

5 How long did it take to *get used to/be used to* eating late or maybe you *didn't use to/aren't used to* it yet?

6 We *used to/'re used to* write letters by hand, but since then I've got *used to/'m used to* doing everything on the computer.

7 Before my divorce my wife *would/was used to* cook all my meals, and I'm still not *used to/getting used to* doing things for myself.

8 Are you getting used to *wear/wearing* a uniform? What did you *use/used* to wear in your last school?

4 ▶ 3.2 Listen to the phrases and underline the main stress in each sentence. Then listen and repeat.

1 I used to love it.

2 I didn't use to discuss it.

3 We'd always eat together.

4 We'd always argue.

5 He's not used to it yet.

6 I'm getting used to it.

7 She can't get used to it.

8 I've got used to it.

5 Complete the forum answers with the correct forms of *used to*, *would*, *be used to* or *get used to* and, where necessary, the verb in brackets. There may be more than one possibility.

👍 Friends   ✏ Add a note   ⏱ Time   ⚙ Holidays   📖 Books

Do you find it easy to get used to change?

JonB: We moved to Canada earlier this year and we've found it difficult to ^{1}_____ the cold winters – before then we ^{2}_____ (live) in New Mexico. The best piece of advice I was given was to invest in a very warm coat and hat!

Alex: Two months ago my doctor told me I needed to eat less salt. Up to then I ^{3}_____ (put) about a spoonful of salt on a lot of things I ate. I ^{4}_____ (think) food was tasteless without it. It was difficult at first but now I ^{5}_____ it and whenever we eat out the food tastes too salty.

Vicki2012: We've got a new baby. Just two weeks old. We love him to bits but he doesn't sleep at night. We ^{6}_____ (have) at least eight hour's sleep. Now we're lucky if we get two hours before he wakes us up. People say 'You'll ^{7}_____ (sleep) for short periods,' but so far I haven't.

ChloeOK: I've just started my first job after university, and it's been a shock to the system! At university I ^{8}_____ (get up) at about nine o'clock and now I have to be at work at nine. I can't ^{9}_____ (wake up) at six. I'm still half asleep when I'm on the train to work!

NewHubby: I got married last month, and we've moved into our first flat. I ^{10}_____ (live) alone, so it's strange for me to share everything with someone, even my wife. Before, I ^{11}_____ (wash up) whenever I wanted to, but my wife hates the mess, so I have to do it right away. I have no choice but to ^{12}_____ it to keep her happy.

LEARN TO use linkers in an opinion essay

6A Read the opinion essay. Which paragraph develops the positive side (P) of the argument, and which two paragraphs develop the negative (N)?

A lifelong partner should be someone who has similar values, personality and interests. Do you agree?

1 Can you imagine being married to someone who is very different from you, in terms of their personality, beliefs or interests? In my view, it would be a recipe for disaster!

2 a) I believe it is vital that two people in a long-term relationship share the same basic values. b) If one of you believes that it is acceptable to read the other person's diary or emails and the other one doesn't, this could cause real problems.

3 c) I feel it is important that people have similar personalities and interests. d) Imagine you are an extrovert person who loves going out but you are married to someone who prefers to spend their evenings at home. Or e) consider a situation where one of you spends hours on their hobby but neglects their partner. The resulting tensions could put a serious strain on the relationship.

4 f) It is true that people can learn a lot from their differences. g) An outgoing person might help their shyer partner become more comfortable in social situations, and therefore have more varied experiences than they might otherwise. This can lead to both people developing much more than they might if both of them were similar.

5 h) Although it is said that 'opposites attract', it seems to me that the basis of a long-lasting relationship is having similar ideas, personalities and interests.

B Complete the essay with the linkers in the box. Write a)–h) next to the appropriate linker. Some can go in more than one position.

---

to sum up,   for example,   as another example,
at the same time,   in addition to this,   furthermore,
to start with,   for instance, (x2)

C Write an opinion essay (200–250 words) on the following topic.

A true friendship is hard work.

SPACE TOURISM IS HERE!

1 Fed up with the usual week-long holiday on the beach, or walking through museums and old buildings that you only pretend to be interested in? Well, consider the ultimate in niche tourism: a new frontier, 'the final frontier' in fact: space tourism.

2 It wasn't long ago that space hotels were the stuff of science fiction, and space tourism was a concept that only the craziest of business entrepreneurs talked about seriously. But since the 2001 flight of Dennis Tito, an American businessman, aboard a Russian Soyuz rocket, even sceptics have had to regard space tourism as an area with real commercial potential. In the first few years, a space tourist like Tito paid $20 million for a trip which included a week-long stay on the International Space Station.

3 It was only a matter of time before the entrepreneurs got on the case, and UK entrepreneur Sir Richard Branson and his Virgin Galactic company have begun offering online bookings for sub-orbital flights aboard their SpaceShipTwo. Tickets start at $200,000, but are expected to come down in price to somewhere around $20,000 – almost a bargain compared to what Tito paid. But the Virgin flights are only two-and-a-half hours, taking passengers just beyond the 100-kilometre altitude that is the internationally defined boundary between earth and space. Space tourists experience a few minutes of weightlessness and a view of the stars before heading back to earth and gliding in for a landing. A German company has been working on providing a similar service called Project Enterprise.

4 What about accommodation? A number of companies have come up with plans to develop space hotels that can offer more luxurious surroundings than the International Space Station, which was designed for research purposes, not for tourists. The Space Island Group planned a ring-shaped spacecraft much like the one in the film *2001: A Space Odyssey*, and situated about 640 kilometres from earth. The ring would rotate in order to create a gravitational pull, so that tourists don't spend

their space holiday floating in the air. Galactic Suite Ltd was at one point targeting 2012 as the opening date for its luxury space hotel, with three-night stays going for $4.4 million – but that includes six weeks of training! And at least one international hotel chain has also expressed an intention of getting into the space hotel business.

5 So is there a hope for ordinary folk who have run out of earthly destinations for their holidays but can't afford the going price for a seat on SpaceShipTwo or a few nights at The Galactic Suite Space Resort? Space enthusiasts are optimistic, and encourage any would-be space tourist to keep saving up and expect prices to keep coming down as competition gets more vicious. And for those who can't dream of putting together the money to meet the price tag, there's always the prospect, however unlikely, of getting a job in one of the space hotels. How does that sound for a year working abroad?

READING

1A Read the article quickly and write the paragraph number next to topics a)–e).

a) more recent developments

b) history and background

c) why you should read the article

d) space tourism for people who aren't rich

e) space hotels

B Read the article again and write true (T), false (F) or not given (NG) next to sentences 1–8. Underline the part of the article that helped you.

1 The writer thinks that business entrepreneurs are crazy.

2 Dennis Tito spent a week in space.

3 The Virgin Galactic flights stop at a space station but don't stay overnight.

4 The writer thinks that Tito should have bargained better.

5 The International Space Station doesn't have very luxurious facilities.

6 The Galactic Suite space hotel rotates to create gravity.

7 Some people think commercial space travel will be more and more competitive.

8 The writer recommends getting a job as an air steward or stewardess.

C Find a word/phrase in the article that means:

1 the kind of thing that something is made of (paragraph 2) _____

2 people who doubt whether something is true or right (paragraph 2) _____

3 started thinking about how to solve a problem (paragraph 3) _____

4 following a path which does not go fully around the earth (paragraph 3) _____

5 thought of (paragraph 4) _____

6 aiming at (paragraph 4) _____

7 the normal cost (paragraph 5) _____

8 aggressive (paragraph 5) _____

GRAMMAR future forms review

2 Correct the mistakes in the underlined phrases. Two are correct.

A: Sue ¹will take a year off from work, but she hasn't decided yet.

B: What ²is she doing if she does take the year off?

A: She said she ³'s thinking to travel a bit.

A: Look, they say there ⁴'s likely to be bad weather tomorrow.

B: I suppose they ⁵'re postponing the outdoor concert then.

A: Maybe so. I ⁶'m phoning and asking before we ⁷will leave.

A: Their boat ⁸gets in just after nine.

B: So when ⁹are we going eating?

A: After they ¹⁰will arrive, I guess.

3 Rewrite the sentences using the words in brackets. Do not change the form of the word.

1 It will probably be hot tomorrow. (likely)

It _____

_____ .

2 Chris wants to find a new job. (hoping)

Chris _____

_____ .

3 I want to see Ingrid and then I'll leave. (before)

I _____

_____ .

4 They're meeting at 3 o'clock tomorrow. (planning)

They _____

_____ .

5 Barcelona are certain to win the championship. (definitely)

Barcelona _____

_____ .

6 You're finishing early? Call me right away. (as soon as)

Call _____

_____ .

7 There's a good chance that she'll get her work permit tomorrow. (well)

She _____

_____ .

8 I'm not likely to see you tomorrow. (probably)

I _____

_____ .

VOCABULARY locations

4A Add vowels to complete the phrases describing locations.

The stunning Dingle ¹P__n__ns__l__ , sticking out into the Atlantic Ocean, is one of the most ²r__m__t__ and ³__nsp__ __lt regions in Ireland. Only 320 km from Dublin ⁴__s th__ cr__w fl__ __s, it is famous for its 2,000 archeological sites and is one of the least ⁵d__ns__ly p__p__l__t__d areas in the country. If you like walking, visit Castlegregory (population 205!), located on the north coast ⁶h__lf-w__y b__tw__ __n Tralee and Dingle, and wander on the sandy beaches along the water's ⁷__dg__. Or why not try climbing the ⁸sl__p__s of Mount Brandon, the second-highest mountain in Ireland. From its ⁹s__mm__t, you can enjoy stunning views of the Blasket Islands, a tiny group of uninhabited islands just ¹⁰__ff th__ south-west c__ __st. However, due to its ¹¹cl__s__ pr__x__m__ty to the Atlantic, weather conditions can change suddenly, so make sure you are warmly dressed!

B Read the text and find:

1 why it can rain suddenly there

_____

2 a completely unpopulated place

_____

3 the location of some ruins

_____

4 the location of a small village

_____

VOCABULARY *PLUS* uncountable and plural nouns

5 Complete the crossword.

Across

2 a 4-star hotel has more of these, and they're better

4 a place to sleep or stay for a while

5 what's left of an ancient building

9 e.g., in sport, a tennis racquet, golf clubs

10 all the things in your bag

Down

1 suitcases

3 everything you find out when you ask questions

6 the view of natural features, for example out of a train window

7 suggestions

8 _____ of transport

FUNCTION describing procedures

1A Complete the rules for the game with the phrases in the box.

what usually happens	after	way	the first thing	basically	
key thing	the point	object			

The ¹_____ it works is that you draw a grid of 5x5 on a piece of paper. There are two players, and the ²_____ of the game is to complete the sequence 'SOS' in a straight line as many times as you can. So ³_____ you do is one of you writes an 'S' or an 'O' in one of the squares. Then the other player writes an 'S' or an 'O' in another square. Whenever one of you completes an 'SOS', you get another turn and ⁴_____, ⁵_____ is not to let your partner succeed, so ⁶_____ is that one player gets an 'SOS' and then blocks the other player. It's easy to lose track of who's winning so the ⁷_____ is to keep score of who gets how many 'SOSs'. Then ⁸_____ you've finished (once the grid is full), the winner is the player with the most 'SOSs'.

B ▶ 3.3 Listen and check your answers.

VOCABULARY common actions

2 Find ten common actions in the word search.

D	O	U	B	L	E	C	L	I	C	K
U	A	M	H	J	S	T	I	R	A	E
N	Y	S	P	R	I	N	K	L	E	X
P	R	S	R	D	E	A	L	O	U	T
L	O	T	E	G	V	T	C	E	U	S
U	L	F	S	L	E	A	N	D	E	E
G	L	F	S	F	Q	J	A	M	C	I

3 Complete the sentences with the correct form of the words in Exercise 2.

1 Don't throw the ball to the baby, _____ it along the floor to her. She can't catch yet.

2 You should _____ your tea or else the sugar will just stay at the bottom.

3 Look, there's no power because someone has _____ it from the wall.

4 First you shuffle the cards, then you _____ them _____.

5 I _____ the reset button but nothing happened.

6 The window's broken so you'll need to _____ it open with a piece of wood.

7 He felt unwell and had to _____ on his wife to keep from collapsing.

8 They _____ the soil to get the stones out, then planted the seeds in it.

9 _____ on the icon to open the programme.

10 It's not very sweet so you might want to _____ a little sugar on top.

LEARN TO use mirror questions

4A Complete the mirror questions to check the words/phrases in italics.

1 **A:** Look up the idiom *under the key word.*
   B: *Look up the idiom where?*

2 **A:** You should see *the deputy director.*
   B: _____?

3 **A:** I last spoke to her *on Christmas Eve.*
   B: _____?

4 **A:** You can use a question word *to clarify.*
   B: _____?

5 **A:** *The cast* is waiting backstage.
   B: _____?

6 **A:** The rain's *lashing down.*
   B: _____?

7 **A:** You'll find us *in the green room.*
   B: _____?

8 **A:** The *lectern* is too high.
   B: _____?

B ▶ 3.4 Listen and check your answers.

C Listen again and underline the main stressed word in each question.

D Listen and repeat, paying attention to the stress and intonation.

Look up the idiom where?

GRAMMAR narrative tenses

1A Underline the correct alternative.

1 One day the old man *fished/was fishing* as usual when he *saw/was seeing* something shiny in the water.

2 In 1995 Ella *was teaching/taught* in the Sudan and *became/had become* well known locally as the 'Canadian lady'.

3 I *'d known/'d been knowing* Javier for many years and when I *read/was reading* he was in prison I knew there must be a mistake.

4 He *noticed/was noticing* that someone *had left/had been leaving* a briefcase on the park bench.

5 The Prince *had been searching/was searching* in the forest for over ten hours and *began/was beginning* to lose hope.

6 Ella *had looked/had been looking* through old photo albums all morning when she *heard/was hearing* a knock on the door, and that moment inspired the lyrics to her greatest hit.

7 By that evening the children *were/had been* exhausted and hungry because they *'d walked/'d been walking* in the forest all day with nothing to eat.

8 We *'d driven/'d been driving* 30 km when the engine suddenly stopped; someone *took/had taken* most of the petrol out of the car, someone who wanted us dead.

B Which of the sentences above do you think come from: a detective story (D), a traditional folk tale (F) or a biography of someone's life (B)?

2 Complete the sentences with the past perfect or the past perfect continuous form of the verbs in brackets. If both are possible, use the past perfect continuous.

1 In the morning everything was white because it _____ (snow) all night.

2 'How long _____ (the victim/come) to this club?' Logan asked.

3 My brother was furious because I _____ (break) his MP3 player.

4 How much money _____ (you/make) by the time you were twenty?

5 I had a sore throat because I _____ (sing) all evening.

6 _____ (she/ever/do) anything like that before?

7 They _____ (not/plan) to move, but a flat became available suddenly.

8 The computer _____ (make) strange noises since the installation of new software.

3A Complete the news story with the correct form of the verbs in the box. There may be more than one possibility.

fail	rush	begin	bring	feel	realise	sit	seem
overhear	explain	climb	use	change	tell		

SPIDER-MAN SAVES THE DAY

An eight-year-old boy has been rescued by an enterprising Bangkok firefighter.

The boy from Thailand is autistic* and ¹_____ very nervous before his first day of school but initially he ²_____ to be OK. However, during the first lesson his teacher ³_____ something to the class when she ⁴_____ that the boy ⁵_____ out of the window. 'He ⁶_____ just outside the window with his legs swinging over the edge.'

The rescue services were called in when the boy's mother ⁷_____ (also) to get the boy down. Everyone ⁸_____ to run out of ideas when one of the firefighters, Somchai Yoosabai, ⁹_____ the boy's mother talking about her son's love of superheroes. The quick-thinking fireman ¹⁰_____ back to the fire station and ¹¹_____ into his Spider-Man costume. (Until then, Mr Somchai ¹²_____ the costume to make school fire drills more interesting.) 'I ¹³_____ him, "Spider-Man is here to rescue you, no monsters are going to attack you."' The sight ¹⁴_____ a smile to the youngster's face and he immediately walked into his rescuer's arms.

*a person who is autistic has a learning disability; it's difficult for them to communicate and form relationships

B ▶ 4.1 Listen to the news story above. For each verb 1–14 underline the main stressed syllable and write any weak forms: (/ə/ or /ɪ/).

C Listen again and read the news story at the same time as the speaker. Pay attention to the stress and weak forms in the verbs.

LISTENING

4A ▶ 4.2 **According to research, there are only seven types of stories or 'plots'. Match plots 1–7 with descriptions a)–g). Then listen and check your ideas.**

1 overcoming the monster

2 rags to riches

3 the quest

4 voyage and return

5 comedy

6 tragedy

7 rebirth

a) The hero/heroine goes on a long, dangerous journey to achieve a goal.

b) A hero/heroine defeats a terrifying beast and saves others or wins a reward.

c) After misunderstandings and confusion, everything ends happily. It doesn't have to be funny but it often is.

d) A person leaves home and goes to a strange place. After adventures, he/she comes back.

e) Someone is in a terrible situation and then returns to happiness or is freed, often by the power of love.

f) An ordinary person discovers special talents or beauty in himself/herself, and often gains great wealth.

g) A character follows a course of action which destroys him/her. This story always has a bad ending.

B Listen again. Which plot are the following connected to?

1 computer games _____

2 Superman _____

3 Romeo and Juliet _____

4 detective stories _____

5 humour _____

6 *Lost* _____

7 losing money _____

VOCABULARY sayings

5 Complete the sayings. Use the prompts to help you.

1 The company has survived previous disasters. So *where / life / hope*
   where there's life there's hope.

2 If we buy a car we may not be able to afford a holiday but *cross / bridge / come / it* _____ .

3 We may fail but we won't know unless we try. As they say, '*Nothing / venture / gain*' _____

4 Sue lost her job recently but *cloud / silver / lining* and now she's got a better one. _____ .

5 Li always gave money to a beggar, and one day the beggar saved him from a mugger. It's certainly true that *go / around / come / around* _____

6 I'm learning to bargain in markets. I've decided *Rome / do / Romans / do* _____ .

7 No more second-hand computers for me – this one keeps breaking down. *Once / bite / twice / shy* _____

8 They only caught two students cheating but I'm sure many more do. After all, *where / smoke / fire* _____ .

LEARN TO use adverbs

6A Read the story. Which saying 1–3 does the story illustrate?

1 Every cloud has a silver lining.

2 What goes around comes around.

3 Once bitten twice shy.

THE LION AND THE MOUSE

Once, as a lion was sleeping, a mouse passed by and [1]_____ woke him up; [2]_____ the lion was angry and wanted to eat the mouse. The mouse [3]_____ said she was very sorry and promised to help the lion in the future. The lion laughed [4]_____ at this, and let her go, because she had made him laugh.

Months later, [5]_____ the mouse got her chance to help the lion when he was tied to a tree by some hunters. When the lion roared, [6]_____ the mouse was nearby and came running. She tried to eat through the rope; it was very thick, but [7]_____ she ate through it [8]_____ and freed the lion. And the moral of the story is …

B Complete the story in Exercise 6A with adverbs from the box or adverbs of your own.

stupidly	fortunately	naturally
eventually	immediately	finally
completely	loudly	

C Use the notes below to write the story (80–100 words). Use at least three adverbs from Exercise 6B to make your story more interesting.

The crow and the water pot: thirsty crow – find – water pot – water at the bottom – can't reach; at first – stare at pot – try to think what to do; clever plan – drop – small stones – one by one – water rise – top – crow drink; moral: 'Necessity is the mother of invention.'

GRAMMAR *I wish; If only; should have*

1A Complete the survey results with the correct form of the verbs in brackets. In some sentences you need to make either the auxiliary or the main verb negative.

| HOME | NEWS | SURVEY | SEARCH |

Regrets, we've had a few ...

A survey of over-30s suggests that many people share the same regrets about the past. Some of the results are unsurprising but others are unexpected. The top regrets are:

■ One in ten people wishes they ¹_____ abroad at some stage in their life. (work)

■ Just under a quarter of people wish they ²_____ more money in their twenties. (save)

■ A quarter of people wished they ³_____ smoking. (begin)

■ Nearly a third of people wished they ⁴_____ more attention at school. (pay)

■ One in three people thinks that they should ⁵_____ so young. (get married)

■ Many people believe they should ⁶_____ full-time education so early and regret that they didn't go to university. (leave)

■ Almost a half of people wish they ⁷_____ a musical instrument. (learn)

■ The top regret of all? Nearly half of people say they should ⁸_____ more when they were younger. (travel)

B Tick the items you regret now or think you will regret in the future.

2A ▶ 4.3 Listen and underline the alternative you hear.

1 I wish *I had/I'd had* more money.

2 I wish *I'd/you'd* worked harder at school.

3 I wish *it would stop/it had stopped* raining.

4 I *should have/shouldn't have* told her.

5 We *should have/shouldn't have* gone to the party.

6 You *should have/shouldn't have* turned it off.

B Listen again and repeat. Pay attention to the stress, the contractions: *'d* /əd/, *hadn't* /ˈhædənt/ and the weak forms: *should have* /ʃʊdəv/, *shouldn't have* /ʃʊdəntəv/.

3 Complete the second sentence so that it has a similar meaning to the first. Use between two and five words including the word given.

1 She can't stand the way the press keep asking her about her private life.

STOP

She wishes the press _____ about her private life.

2 I'd prefer to be at home right now; it's too cold here.

HOME

I wish _____ right now; it's too cold here.

3 It's terrible – we owe so much money!

ONLY

If _____ so much money.

4 They didn't tell him the cost before he started the treatment.

TOLD

He should _____ the cost before he started the treatment.

5 I hate it when you interrupt me.

ME

I wish _____.

6 That's a great idea! Why didn't I think of it?

WISH

I _____ of that idea.

7 Wayne wishes he'd kept his temper.

SHOULDN'T

Wayne _____ his temper.

8 I can't see anything from here.

SEE

If only _____ from here.

9 Unfortunately, we don't have enough time.

MORE

If _____ time.

10 You just didn't listen to me!

LISTENED

You _____ to me!

VOCABULARY regrets

4 Put the letters in bold in the correct order. The first letter is underlined.

1 Beckham injury a terrible **tyip**, says coach   *pity*

2 PM having **docens shuttgoh** about re-election, may withdraw

3 Bankers **cikk sleemvesht** over bad investment

4 Report: With **shigthdin**, plane crash avoidable

5 Climate Change Conference a **sedsim pipyrotunot** say critics

6 Celebrity **detugt** about stolen Porsche

READING

5A Read the article and answer the questions.

1 What is the challenge each person faces?

2 How do they manage in their professions?

Our series on people who have achieved success in their field in the face of extraordinary challenges.

For more than thirty years, soprano Janine Roebuck has delighted audiences with her singing in opera and musical theatre. For most of that time she has kept a closely guarded secret: she is profoundly deaf.

Janine comes from a family with hereditary deafness. At first she thought she had escaped the disability but at university she was diagnosed with progressive loss of hearing and was advised to give up her dream of a singing career. However, Janine decided to hide the truth from fellow musicians. 'I was terrified. I thought that if people knew that I was deaf, they would see me as a liability and not employ me.' She developed coping strategies to enable her to perform. When she sang with another person she watched their breathing so that she could come in at the right time. She felt vibrations from the music, and occasionally she asked her fellow performers to tap the beat on her back.

Now Janine has decided to reveal the truth. 'I'm proud of what I've achieved and I want to encourage other people.' As the word about Janine's deafness spreads, responses include astonishment and admiration. And her proudest moment? 'One conductor told his orchestra I was deaf only after they'd heard me sing. Their standing ovation is the reaction I treasure the most.'

If you listen to Dean Du Plessis on the radio you will hear an articulate sports commentator with a comprehensive knowledge of cricket. It's incredible then to realise that Zimbabwean Du Plessis has never actually seen a game because he has been blind from birth.

How does he do it? He says his heightened sense of hearing compensates for his lack of sight. He uses microphones placed around the ground to help. 'I can tell the players by the sounds they make when they hit the ball or they run up the pitch. Some people drag their feet or make a particular grunting sound when they use a lot of effort.' He also listens to the sounds when the bat strikes the ball, as well as the crowd.

Born near Harare, Zimbabwe, Du Plessis was lucky enough to attend the famous Worcester School for the Blind in South Africa. At school, much to the annoyance of his schoolmates, he would stay up late in the evening and do commentaries alongside the radio. 'Then one evening a teacher came up to me and said, "Dean, you should take this up as a profession, because you're brilliant!"'

In 2001 Dean tried out with the microphone at Harare Sports Club and since then has never looked back. His passion and knowledge make him enormously popular with listeners and leave visiting teams and his co-commentators awestruck.

B Who do you think said the following: Janine (J) or Dean (D)?

1 It was a terrible blow to me.

2 It can be a sharp crack or a quieter sound.

3 Until then I thought I was one of the lucky ones.

4 Your other senses become more acute.

5 I refused to give up.

6 Why now? Well with age you don't really care so much.

7 Maybe they didn't like my style. Or they just wanted to sleep.

8 I don't miss it because I've never known anything different.

C Try to complete the collocations below. Then read the text again to check your ideas.

1 a _____ secret = a well-kept secret

2 _____ deaf = very deaf

3 to _____ a strategy = to invent and improve on a technique

4 to _____ the truth = to tell the truth after hiding it

5 a _____ knowledge = a complete knowledge

6 a _____ sense of hearing = increased sense of hearing

VOCABULARY PLUS
multi-word verbs

6A Complete the questions in the interview by adding *down, off, on, over, to* or *up*.

A: So you were brought ¹_____ by the ocean?

B: Yes, when I was growing ²_____ I practically lived underwater.

A: And when you started taking photos, you took ³_____ it quickly?

B: Yeah, I loved it *and* I was good at it so after school I went ⁴_____ to look for a job that combined my two great loves.

A: But you were turned ⁵_____ by all the local companies. Do you think they were put ⁶_____ by your lack of experience?

B: Probably. Anyway, as time went ⁷_____ I began to think I'd never get a job.

A: Why do you think Global took you ⁸_____ in such a key position then?

B: They didn't, not at first. I was only an assistant on a documentary.

A: So did your boss step ⁹_____ from his position?

B: No … he was badly injured by a shark. Shocking stuff.

A: Oh, I'm sorry. How long did you take to get ¹⁰_____ that?

B: I never have, to be honest. But now I get all the big films.

B What is person B's job?

VOCABULARY reading

1 Complete the crossword.

Across

1 A book that tells you how to do something, especially how to use a machine.

4 A type of website containing information or opinions from a particular person or about a particular subject. New information or comments are added regularly.

6 An electronic version of a printed book which is read on a a computer or a specially designed hand-held device.

7 An online _____ has facts and information about many different subjects.

8 A website where people take part in online discussions.

10 A _____ magazine is about the behaviour and private lives of famous people.

11 Poems in general.

Down

2 A written story about fictional characters.

3 A book that someone writes about their own life.

4 The story someone writes about someone else's life.

5 The words of a song.

9 Japanese comics, often action-adventure, which are read by all ages.

FUNCTION expressing likes and dislikes

2A Complete B's part in each conversation.

A: What did you think of the book?

B: ¹Well, / not / big fan / travel books

_____

A: Oh, why's that?

B: ²I / not / that keen / all the description

_____

A: I hear Nick's enjoying his new school.

B: ³Yes, what / he / love / about it / be / that they do / lot of sport

_____

A: I didn't know he liked sport.

B: ⁴Oh, yeah. / He / be / really into football / moment

_____

A: Why don't you like barbecues?

B: ⁵not / stand / when the meat / not / cooked properly

_____

A: You haven't tasted *my* barbecues!

B: ⁶And / other thing / hate / about them / be / the mosquitoes

_____

A: OK. Maybe we'd better stay inside.

B ▶ 4.4 Listen and check your answers.

C ▶ 4.5 Listen and underline between two and five main stresses in B's part.

D Listen again and say B's part at the same time as the recording.

LEARN TO summarise a plot

3 Complete the plot summary with the correct form of the verbs in the box.

wait	fall (x2)	deliver	die	have	work	earn
meet (x2)	kick out (x2)					

As is true of many of his stories, there is an autobiographical element, with the life of the main character, Irek, bearing many resemblances to that of the author, André Hartowicz. In real life, Hartowicz, a political activist, ¹_____ of university for organising protests against the administration. In the novel, the main character ²_____ of university for signing a letter criticising the examination system. Hartowicz, before he became famous, ³_____ as a waiter to pay his rent; in the story, Irek ⁴_____ money as a postman.

Hartowicz ⁵_____ his first wife at a restaurant; she ⁶_____ dinner with her husband while Hartowicz ⁷_____ on tables, and they ⁸_____ in love at first sight. In the story, however, Irek ⁹_____ his wife-to-be when he ¹⁰_____ a letter to her informing her that her husband ¹¹_____ in battle. They too ¹²_____ in love at first sight.

1 Complete the story with the correct form of the verbs in brackets. There may be more than one possibility.

20 Monday

It was May 1997 and I ¹_____ (think) it was going to be the last day of my life.

I ²_____ (study) archaeology in Greece with twelve other students for two months before that. We ³_____ (come) towards the end of our trip – there were only five days left, and that day we ⁴_____ (look) at the underwater ruins of an ancient town off the beach at Pavlopetri.

As I recall, the ruins were about two hundred metres off the beach. It ⁵_____ (rain) the night before and the water was still cool. Only half of us at a time ⁶_____ (swim) out to the ruins because we ⁷_____ (share) masks and snorkels, and taking turns to look at the ruins. After a while I ⁸_____ (begin) to feel tired and cold, so I ⁹_____ (tell) my friend Mike that I ¹⁰_____ (go) back to the beach. About halfway back to the beach, still in two-metre-deep water, I ¹¹_____ (realise) I was in trouble: I was very cold, I couldn't move my arms and I ¹²_____ (go) in and out of consciousness.

Fortunately, minutes earlier, Mike ¹³_____ (realise) that something was wrong. He was a qualified lifeguard and he got me to the beach but by then I ¹⁴_____ (shake) uncontrollably from hypothermia. Everyone ¹⁵_____ (massage) me to make me warm and only stopped when I ¹⁶_____ (recover).

2 Complete the sentences with the correct word/phrase.

1 neglected/ignored
   a) Eric simply _____ all the complaints from his lodgers.
   b) Increasingly, Naomi _____ her work because of all her other responsibilities.

2 complimented/paid attention
   a) Ali _____ his brother on his promotion.
   b) Sam _____ whenever his wife gave him good advice.

3 take care/get on
   a) Noriko will _____ of all the administrative details.
   b) You can _____ with the work as soon as you arrive.

4 selfish/stubborn
   a) You can be so _____! You know you were wrong; you should say sorry.
   b) That was a very _____ thing to do. You never think of anyone else.

5 hindsight/second thoughts
   a) Gregor had _____ about getting married.
   b) With _____ he realized he should never have taken the job.

6 gutted/kicked
   a) I was _____ because I failed the exam.
   b) I _____ myself because I hadn't spoken when I had the chance.

7 take to/take up
   a) Danni has just started piano lessons. We're hoping he'll _____ it.
   b) I'm planning to _____ running next year.

8 taken on/set up
   a) The company has _____ more than fifty new workers.
   b) We have _____ a number of new business centres in major cities.

9 in close proximity/on the edge
   a) We wanted to find a house _____ to the lake.
   b) The houses that were _____ of the lake were too expensive.

3A Look at the underlined sounds in each group. Circle the word with the different sound.

1 bi<u>o</u>graphy, h<u>i</u>ndsight, prox<u>i</u>mity
2 crit<u>i</u>cise, s<u>ie</u>ve, l<u>y</u>rics,
3 ign<u>ore</u>, aut<u>o</u>biography, cl<u>ou</u>d
4 gener<u>ous</u>, s<u>u</u>mmit, d<u>ou</u>ble-click
5 encyclop<u>e</u>dia, p<u>i</u>ty, l<u>ea</u>n
6 opp<u>or</u>tunity, stub<u>bor</u>n, f<u>o</u>rested

B ▶ RC2.1 Listen and check. Then listen and repeat.

GRAMMAR future forms review

4 Complete the articles with an appropriate future form of one of the verbs. There may be more than one possibility.

| use | become | be likely | think |

All charged up?

1_____ you _____ of buying an electric car but are worried about the amount of time it takes to charge the batteries? All that 2_____ to change thanks to a discovery by scientists in the USA. The new batteries 3_____ lithium iron phosphate and 4_____ available within two years.

| start | not keep | lose | break |

This year … or maybe next?

Happy New Year! Now the bad news: three out of four of us 5_____ our New Year resolutions by the end of January. Even worse, a quarter of us 6_____ our promises until the end of week one. 'People's intentions are always good,' says the manager of a nation-wide chain of gyms, 'They say they 7_____ weight and get fit, but as soon as it 8_____ to get difficult, they give up.'

| plan | ask | take off | meet |

interview

Saturday

It's 5.45a.m. and I'm sitting in a hotel lobby, waiting to interview the richest man in the world. We 9_____ at 6 o'clock for a twenty-minute breakfast. At exactly 6.30a.m. his helicopter 10_____ from the hotel roof so I'm lucky to get even twenty minutes of his time. I 11_____ to ask him about his charity work and if there's time, I 12_____ him about the recent scandal.

VOCABULARY uncountable and plural nouns

5 Add -s in seven places and remove it in seven places. Make any other necessary changes to the spelling.

TRAVEL

There is a maximum weight of twenty kilos for passengers' luggages. Security is strict at the airport and you will be asked to confirm that no one has interfered with the content of your bags. The airport is situated on the outskirt of the city and there are several mean of transports to get to the city centre. We recommend the airport bus as it is cheaper and more reliable than the taxis. Full informations about your accommodations can be found on our website. Note that all hotels are three-star and have facility such as laundry, TV in every room, and internet access. Electricities voltage is 220V and you will need an adaptor or European plug.

TOURS

Tours are available daily and include a visit to the remain of the old city a few kilometres to the north and a visit to the desert in the south, with stunning view from the bus of the spectacular sceneries. There will be an opportunity to meet some of the local and buy their handmade goods. We will also visit the approximate site of the tombs of the kings although their exact whereabout are not known.

GRAMMAR used to, would, be/get used to

6 Complete B's answers with the words in the box.

| didn't wasn't would weren't work can't got ~~to~~ |

A: Do you mind people asking you about your childhood?

B: ¹No, I'm used to it.

A: So, did you always want to be a singer?

B: ²Yes. From the age of four I dress up and sing for my parents.

A: But after their divorce, you were brought up by your grandparents?

B: ³That's right, but they used to having children around so I was sent away to school, which I hated. ⁴I used to sitting still for so long.

A: But you did well in the end, didn't you?

B: ⁵Yes, eventually I used to the routine and I worked hard.

A: Did anyone recognise your talent at that point?

B: ⁶No, I use to enjoy the music classes and so I hardly ever joined in. But then we got a new teacher. ⁷He used to for a music publisher, and he put my song *Sampling Love* on the internet.

A: And as they say, the rest is history.

B: ⁸Yes, I still get used to it.

FUNCTION describing procedures

7 Correct the mistakes in the underlined phrases.

A great steak makes a quick, tasty meal but is hard to get right. ¹The first thing you do is making sure the steak is the right temperature. If it is frozen, then defrost it overnight. ²A point is to make sure the meat is at room temperature so that it cooks well throughout.

³The next pre-heat a heavy griddle pan over a high heat. ⁴Key thing is to ensure the pan is sufficiently hot, but not smoking or the steak will be cooked unevenly. Meanwhile season the meat and brush it with a little oil. Put the meat in the pan and ⁵after that you've cooked one side, turn it over. ⁶The main thing is keep turning it or it can dry out.

⁷Basic, the object is to keep the meat full of flavour, so never cut it to check if it's cooked. Right at the end, press the steak gently with your finger: rare should be soft, well done firm and medium in between. ⁸After, remove the steak from the pan, cover it with foil and 'rest' it for a few minutes. ⁹ The way it work is that then the juices can run back through the steak. ¹⁰What it happens next is up to you. You can serve it with potatoes or salad or accompany it with a sauce. **Enjoy!**

FUNCTION likes and dislikes

8 Complete the opinions with the words in the box.

a	~~on~~	not	about	into	the	can't	what

1 I'm really keen ⌃ chillies. They're great for flavouring boring
   on
   dishes.

2 I hate steak when it's rare – I really don't like is the colour.

3 What I like olives is their salty taste, particularly on pizzas.

4 I absolutely stand snails. The thought of them makes me feel sick.

5 I'm really pasta, mainly because it's so quick to make.

6 I'm not big fan of cheese. It's something about the smell.

7 Cherries are my favourite fruit – thing I love about them is their taste.

8 I'm that keen on chocolate as it's often too sweet for me.

GRAMMAR I wish, If only, should have

9 Complete the underlined phrases.

> **chat** online   Search 🔍

News

Gossip

Email

People

What phone and internet mistakes do you wish you could undo?

▶ ¹I should / not post _____
a photo of myself in a swimming costume on a social networking site. When I went for an interview for a job, they'd attached it to my application form!

▶ I once emailed my first girlfriend when I was angry at my wife. ²I / really / wish / I / not _____.
My wife found out and she's never let me forget it.

▶ With hindsight, it was a bad idea to use the James Bond theme tune for my ring tone. ³I / should / choose _____ something more sophisticated.

▶ I sent a joke text message to my boss. Thirty seconds after I'd sent it, I knew ⁴I / should / not _____.
⁵Now / I / wish / I / delete _____ it.

▶ I recently joined a dating website and made the mistake of using a photo of myself from ten years ago. ⁶If only / I / be / as slim as then and / have _____ all my hair again!

▶ I wrote a rude email to a friend and I haven't heard from him since. I hope he emails me soon or ⁷I / wish / he / phone / and / yell / me _____. That would be better than waiting and wondering.

▶ An ex-boyfriend emailed me. Somehow I didn't get round to answering and the next I heard he'd re-married. ⁸If only / I / reply _____ to his email. Maybe we might have got back together.

TEST

Circle the correct option to complete the sentences.

1 When I was young I _____ I could do anything.
   a) used to believe   b) would believe
   c) 'm used to believing

2 Have you read the new _____? It was written by his ex-wife.
   a) gossip   b) biography   c) autobiography

3 Do you ever wish you _____ back in time?
   a) would go   b) went   c) could go

4 If the computer freezes, just _____ it and wait a few minutes.
   a) unplug   b) press   c) jam

5 If only I _____ my flared trousers – they're back in fashion now.
   a) hadn't thrown away   b) could keep
   c) didn't throw away

6 Are you used _____ spicy food?
   a) eat   b) to eat   c) to eating

7 I'm sorry you didn't like what I said, but _____ it!
   a) get over   b) step down from   c) put off

8 Jason and Zena _____ together again after their very public row.
   a) won't probably work   b) probably won't work
   c) won't work probably

9 When _____ the leaflet, can you email it to me immediately?
   a) you finish   b) you will finish
   c) you are finishing

10 We're getting worried because they haven't _____ yet and it's getting dark.
   a) set in   b) turned up   c) settled down

11 Then _____ that microwaves cause the food to vibrate quickly and produce heat.
   a) the thing happens   b) the thing is
   c) what happens is

12 They _____ living with the constant heat.
   a) couldn't get used   b) weren't used to
   c) didn't use to

13 _____ the photo, you can adjust it on your computer.
   a) After you've taken   b) After that you've taken
   c) After that you take

14 Have you found all of the missing _____?
   a) remain   b) equipment   c) outskirts

15 I _____ that I didn't get the job.
   a) 'm having second thoughts   b) with hindsight
   c) 'm gutted

16 How high is the _____ of the mountain?
   a) summit   b) slope   c) edge

17 Whenever I ask him to do something he just _____ me.
   a) neglects   b) ignores   c) doesn't pay attention

18 Stop complaining and just _____ with the job!
   a) don't put off   b) give in   c) get on

19 They _____ the house for an hour when it started raining.
   a) painted   b) had painted   c) had been painting

20 Neela felt relieved because she _____ the speech and could send it off to be checked.
   a) was writing   b) 'd written   c) 'd been writing

21 _____ move your money to another bank?
   a) Are you thinking   b) Are you hoping
   c) Are you planning to

22 What lovely flowers! You _____!
   a) really should   b) shouldn't have
   c) couldn't have

23 In the event of a fire, it will _____ water along the corridors.
   a) sprinkle   b) sieve   c) deal

24 I'd get her some flowers. She's _____ chocolates.
   a) not that keen   b) not a big fan of   c) can't stand

25 Where there's _____, there's _____.
   a) hope/life   b) smoke/fire
   c) a cloud/a silver lining

26 _____ bitten, _____ shy.
   a) Once/twice   b) When/always   c) Once/always

27 The early tribes always lived _____ to the sea.
   a) on a peninsula   b) off the coast
   c) in close proximity

28 I can't put this lawnmower together. Where's the _____?
   a) manual   b) encyclopedia   c) manga

29 _____ I like about the colour is it's so vibrant.
   a) The thing what   b) What   c) It's what

30 How many actors _____ before you chose Rob?
   a) had you seen   b) had you been seeing?
   c) were you seeing

TEST RESULT | **/30**

LISTENING

1A ▶ **5.1** Listen to the radio programme about the Ig Nobel Prize and number the pictures in the order they are mentioned.

B Listen again and complete the descriptions of other Ig Nobel winners.

1 Research into why pregnant women don't _____ over.

2 Research into why dry spaghetti breaks into _____ pieces.

3 A device that makes an annoying noise that only _____ can hear.

4 A business suit that automatically _____ itself.

5 A washing machine for _____ and _____.

C Listen again and circle the best ending, a), b) or c).

1 The name 'Ig Nobel' suggests:
   a) a link to the Nobel prize.
   b) that the prize is 'ignoble' or stupid.
   c) two meanings at the same time.

2 It is awarded for:
   a) ridiculous research and inventions.
   b) amusing but interesting inventions.
   c) potentially major research.

3 The alarm clock was awarded an Ig Nobel prize because:
   a) it was good for the economy.
   b) it helped people get up.
   c) it meant people worked harder.

4 Martha is doing research into:
   a) how to stay dry in the rain.
   b) how people get wet in the rain.
   c) whether an umbrella or a raincoat is better in the rain.

GRAMMAR articles

2 Complete the article with *a(n)*, *the* or – (no article).

An inventor, or the inventor?

It's ¹_____ well-known fact that ²_____ electric light was invented by American Thomas Edison, but is it really true? Edison's light bulb, like many inventions, was ³_____ result of many scientists' work. ⁴_____ English scientist had made ⁵_____ simple electric light seventy years earlier, and Edison's further development of ⁶_____ idea wouldn't have been possible without the work of his colleagues.

Similarly, the Wright brothers are generally credited with inventing the first successful airplane at ⁷_____ beginning of ⁸_____ twentieth century. Yet literally dozens of ⁹_____ inventors and scientists before that time might claim to have taken key steps in developing ¹⁰_____ sustained flight. For instance, ¹¹_____ Norwegian named Navrestad supposedly flew in a glider in 1825, and in subsequent years, ¹²_____ advances were made all over the world. In fact just before the Wright brothers' famous flight, ¹³_____ American named Langley flew over ¹⁴_____ Potomac River, a distance of about 800 metres.

It seems that ¹⁵_____ person who not only achieves a particular feat but also records it, protects it and publicises it will be credited with the discovery.

3 Read the article. Cross out *the* in ten places where it is unnecessary.

$ YOUR **MILLION-DOLLAR** IDEA $

Do you want to join those people who have made a million from a simple idea? Then just follow these five tips:

$ Remember the saying 'necessity is the mother of the invention'. When the people need the things, sooner or later someone will come up with an idea to meet that need. It could be you!

$ Watch people and notice their habits. How do they do the everyday activities, such as answering the phone, handling the money or the credit cards, eating and drinking? Is there a way that one of the activities could be made easier?

$ When you have an idea, write it down. Draw a picture. Give it a name. This will help your mind work on the idea further.

$ Don't talk to the negative people about your ideas. The motivation is important for the creativity, and negative people can kill it.

$ Talk to a friend about your ideas. Some of the most successful ideas emerge through the talking.

VOCABULARY change

4A Complete the puzzle and find a piece of advice.

1. d ▢▢▢▢▢▢▢▢
2. b ▢▢▢▢▢▢▢▢▢
3. ▢▢ v ▢▢▢▢▢▢▢
4. ▢ n ▢▢▢▢
5. d ▢▢▢▢▢
   c
   h
6. t ▢▢▢▢▢▢▢
   n
7. d ▢▢▢▢
8. l ▢▢▢

1 adjective describing a harmful effect
2 adjective describing a positive effect
3 and 6 change something completely
4 make something better
5 change something unnaturally
7 harm
8 make something different

B ▶ 5.2 Listen and check. Then listen again and write the words in the correct column.

Oo	oO	ooOo	ooOoo
		detrimental	

C Listen and repeat.

VOCABULARY *PLUS*

compound nouns

5 Complete the compound nouns with the words in the box.

out	through	off	look	back
down	come	side		

1 Mobile phone access is possible almost everywhere but the down_____ is the increasing number of ugly antennas.

2 One positive out_____ of the availability of electronic media is a decrease in the amount of paper used.

3 The transistor was a major break_____ in the development of electronic devices.

4 In the early days of mobile phones, there was a trade-_____ between battery size and compactness.

5 Long before the barcode, the use of conveyor belts in supermarkets greatly speeded up the processing of customers at the check_____ counter.

6 The biggest draw_____ of the development of electronic communication has been that people see less of each other in person.

7 After the development of atomic weapons, the out_____ for human warfare became depressing and frightening.

8 The use of automated telephone response systems often leads to a communication break_____ between customers and providers.

READING

1A Look at the words in the box. Which do you think are the five best words (B) and which are the five worst words (W) to use in an advertisement?

| Safety | Deal | Quality | Results | Love | Client |
| Discover | Cheap | Health | Best | | |

B Read the article and complete it with the words in the box above.

The ten **best** and **worst** words in advertising

Everyone likes to get something for nothing, but the word 'free' has become **a big no-no** as it's sure to make people think of a product as second-rate. What are the words that are guaranteed to get a result? And what words should advertisers avoid using? Check out the five power words in advertising, and five others that advertisers should delete from their lexicons.

☺ **The top five**

1 _____ – Everybody wants it, everybody needs it, and it's so hard to get; just the mention of it catches people's attention and makes them want the product that seems to promise to deliver.

2 _____ – There's a bit of the explorer in all of us, and while most people are **armchair explorers**, the sense that they are going to experience something new is irresistible.

3 _____ – This has always been important to consumers, but we've seen a clear trend since the 1980s to put physical and mental well-being **at the forefront**. Most people are too busy or lazy to pay attention to their own, and that's all the more reason to make them buy some via your product.

4 _____ – Just a mild suggestion that a product will keep the consumer's family out of danger – particularly if the advertiser can associate the product with protecting children – and most consumers will **dig deeper into their pockets** to pay out.

5 _____ – One advertising psychologist has said that the power of this word is in the association consumers make with their childhood and school; getting good grades was the goal then, and this word makes them think of that. And yes, they still want good ones.

☹ **The bottom five**

6 _____ – Most people will **go to great lengths** to pay less for a product, but this is probably the worst word to communicate that that's what you offer. When it refers to price, it makes the product sound second-rate; unluckily, the word can also refer to quality.

7 _____ – Sure, it's OK to talk about the customer or consumer using this word, but consumers don't like to be referred to in such a technical, business-orientated way.

8 _____ – Similar to 'cheap', this word has associations with tricky used-car salesmen and products that aren't in fact worth spending money on.

9 _____ – Only one product can really be described with this word, and if everyone says theirs is, then who should the consumer believe?

10 _____ – Another word that was once very much in fashion, but overuse has **made** consumers **numb to** its meaning. And who would say their product doesn't have it?

2 Match the meanings 1–6 with the phrases in bold in the article.

1 make extra effort for something you want badly

2 people who dream about doing something, but don't actually do it

3 try hard(er) to get money for something

4 something you should never do

5 a top priority

6 cause people not even to notice

GRAMMAR conditionals

3 Complete the second sentence so that it has a similar meaning to the first. Use between two and five words including the word given.

1 Without more money we can't put an advert on TV.

UNLESS

We can't put an advert on TV
_____ more money.

2 Not many people use the shop because it closes at five o'clock.

LATER

If the shop _____, more people would use it.

3 Could we get a discount by paying in cash?

SUPPOSING

_____ in cash, could we get a discount?

4 Providing we're happy with your work, we'll give you a full-time contract.

LONG

We'll give you a full-time contract
_____ happy with your work.

5 Suppose I accepted the job, how soon would you want me to start?

WERE

If I _____ the job, how soon would you want me to start?

6 If the band were to get back together, would you join it?

BACK

Imagine the band _____, would you join it?

7 I wouldn't go skiing unless I enjoyed it.

SKIING

If I _____, I wouldn't do it.

8 Supposing you didn't go, is there a chance that you would regret it?

MIGHT

_____ if you didn't go?

4 Complete the sentences with the appropriate form of the verbs in brackets.

1 If the shop _____ (not have) the right version, I _____ (get) it online. I haven't decided yet.

2 Supposing Maria _____ (be) here now, what _____ you _____ (say) to her?

3 Good news: you _____ (accept) on the course as long as you _____ (achieve) two A-grades.

4 If I _____ (not be) left-handed, I _____ (not wear) my watch on my right wrist.

5 We _____ (close) the factory unless a buyer _____ (come forward) in the next few days.

6 If Cindy _____ (not know) about the party tomorrow, I think you _____ (tell) her.

7 If I _____ (not sit) here now, I _____ (be) at home playing the guitar.

8 I _____ (buy) you dinner provided that we _____ (pass) the exam!

VOCABULARY advertising

5 Complete the crossword.

Across

2 For example Levis, Apple.

5 A company symbol.

7 A series of advertisements for a product.

9 It's often about thirty seconds long and on TV.

10 A celebrity says a product is good.

11 Another word for 2 across.

Down

1 A sentence that sells a product.

3 Use images and words to sell a product.

4 A short song that sells a product.

6 Make someone think a certain way.

8 Similar to 10 across.

LEARN TO make written comparisons

6A Put the words in the correct order to make phrases for making comparisons.

a) for / less / is / important / far

_____

b) contrast / an / to / show / interesting

_____

c) on / place / importance / greater

_____

d) is / in / no / there / difference / almost

_____

e) equally / both / more / less / affects / groups / or

_____

f) differences / significant / are / there / in

_____

g) a / shows / slight / only / variation

_____

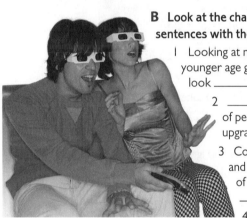

B Look at the chart and complete the sentences with the phrases from Exercise 6A.

1 Looking at men and women in the younger age group, the way the glasses look _____.

2 _____ the number of people who don't have an upgradable TV.

3 Comparing younger men and women, the importance of price and image quality _____.

4 _____ the number of people who watch action films – the films that benefit the most from the 3D effect.

5 Younger men _____ how trendy 3D TV is than the other groups.

6 The results for the older groups _____ those for the younger group.

7 The way the glasses look _____ people in the older age group than the 18-to-25-year-olds.

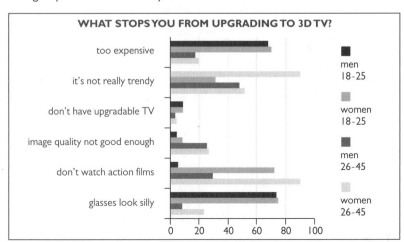

WHAT STOPS YOU FROM UPGRADING TO 3D TV?

- too expensive
- it's not really trendy
- don't have upgradable TV
- image quality not good enough
- don't watch action films
- glasses look silly

0 20 40 60 80 100

- men 18-25
- women 18-25
- men 26-45
- women 26-45

C Write five more sentences about the data in the chart.

FUNCTION suggesting ideas

1A Read the list of ideas. Which two do you think would be the best in your situation?

B Read the conversation. Do the speakers share your ideas?

A: [1]What do you think about simply write writing the rule on a sign on the wall: 'English only'?

B: I think it's too simple. We would ignore it.

C: [2]How much do you feel about a fine system? You have to pay if you speak your language.

B: That's not original enough.

A: [3]I suppose we try a mother-tongue 'island'. A place in the room where you can go to speak your mother tongue if you really need to.

C: That's a terrific idea.

B: [4]It doesn't grab for me.

A: [5]Would you consider about having five-minute mother-tongue breaks in the middle of the lesson?

B: [6]I think we're running on the wrong track here. It's either punishment or reward, nothing else works.

C: [7]How does giving a prize for using only English strike you out? Like no homework? Or chocolate?

B: [8]I'd go agree for that.

A: [9]It'd be great if we should could get more different nationalities in the group. Then we'd naturally speak English more.

B: That's not very realistic.

C: [10]I'm torn up between punishment and reward systems. Fines or prizes.

A: [11]Could we go in for both?

B: Yeah, [12]let's go out with that.

C Cross out the unnecessary word in each underlined phrase.

D ▶ 5.3 Listen to the conversation or read the audio script on page 78 to check.

LEARN TO show reservations

2A Correct the mistake in each sentence.

1 With respectful, we need to be more focussed.

2 To be honestly, I thought your first suggestion was better.

3 To put bluntly, that's the worst idea I've heard today.

4 Actual, I don't think that's a very practical idea.

5 Frankedly, it's just not going to work.

6 As a fact of matter, that's probably the only solution.

B ▶ 5.4 Listen and check. Then listen and repeat, paying attention to the stress and intonation.

VOCABULARY adjectives

3A Complete the words by adding vowels to the adjectives in bold.

1 People who read that won't understand it, they've never heard of any of the people involved – it's too __bsc__r__.

2 When the movie started I already knew how it was going to end. It was so **pr__d__ct__bl__**.

3 They both refused to speak until the other apologised, and so they never spoke again. The situation was totally __bs__rd.

4 Harry's just started at the bank and says he'll be running it within a year. He always was rather __mb__t____s.

5 Hmm … a chicken in a spacesuit … that's **w____rd**.

6 Have you heard? They fired Sophie without warning, and with no pay. It's really **dr____df__l**.

7 So you want to drive two thousand kilometres in two days, all by yourself? I think that's __nr____l__st__c.

8 That's the best idea I've ever heard! It's **br__ll____nt**.

B ▶ 5.5 Listen to the adjectives and circle the correct stress pattern.

1 Oo	oO	5 O	oO
2 oOoo	ooOo	6 Oo	oO
3 Oo	oO	7 oOoo	ooOo
4 Ooo	oOo	8 Oo	oO

VOCABULARY age

1A Correct B's sentences by changing one word.

1 A: I'm going to play on the swings …

   B: Behave your age! They're meant for kids.

2 A: Mina seems very sensible for a sixteen-year-old.

   B: I'm continually surprised by her maternity.

3 A: I can't believe he's seventy!

   B: Yes, he looks very young than his age.

4 A: What are you doing this weekend?

   B: We're visiting an elder aunt of Simon's.

5 A: I think Hugh is too young to become a manager.

   B: Careful – that could be seen as age judgement.

6 A: In her forties, Madonna is attracting even more crowds.

   B: Yes, she's definitely in her time.

7 A: You could say that social networking sites have 'grown up'.

   B: I agree – they've certainly reached of age now.

8 A: I can't believe what he just said!

   B: Yeah, he's so unmature. He really needs to grow up.

B Which age-related phrases in B's responses are positive (✓), negative (-) or neutral (N)?

GRAMMAR modal verbs and phrases

2 Complete the article with the modal verbs and phrases in the box. You do not need to use one of the verbs/phrases.

| can   could   are able   being able to   managed to   couldn't needed   had to   don't have to   are supposed to   made wasn't allowed   obliged to |

WHAT WAS LIFE LIKE BEFORE THE INTERNET?

If you wanted to keep in touch with friends, you [1]_____ just visit a social networking site. You [2]_____ phone or talk to friends face to face.

If you [3]_____ to sell something like a bike, you were [4]_____ put an advert in a local newspaper. These days you [5]_____ to reach thousands of potential buyers through sites such as Craigslist or eBay.

Online encyclopedias didn't exist. As a student, once I only [6]_____ find information for an assignment by spending two days in a library.

Music came from shops in the form of CDs. Nowadays it [7]_____ be downloaded online. Obviously a good thing? Well, you [8]_____ pay for it but many people download illegally.

Before life online, as a kid I was [9]_____ to write long thank-you letters for birthday presents instead of [10]_____ send a quick email. My parents were really strict. I [11]_____ to play with any new toys until I'd written to everyone.

You used to go to friends' homes to watch their holiday videos. Thankfully, you [12]_____ do this anymore. A quick look on a video-sharing site is enough!

3 Complete the second sentence so that it has a similar meaning to the first. Use between two and five words including the word given.

1 There's no obligation for the company to provide training.

   HAVE

   The company _____ training.

2 It's impossible to force kids to eat vegetables.

   MAKE

   You _____ vegetables.

3 We weren't able to see the supervisor.

   MANAGE

   We _____ see the supervisor.

4 He was allowed to go after he'd been questioned for three hours.

   LET

   The police _____ after he'd been questioned for three hours.

5 I'm afraid I can't make the meeting.

   ABLE

   I'm afraid I _____ make the meeting.

6 This area is forbidden. Get out immediately.

   SUPPOSED

   You _____ in this area. Get out immediately.

LISTENING

4A How would you answer questions 1–8?

What's the best age ...

1 **to choose a career?**

2 **to get married?**

3 **to have a baby?**

4 **to start a sport?**

5 **to learn a musical instrument?**

6 **to learn a new language?**

7 **to become president or prime minister?**

8 **to retire?**

B ▶ 6.1 Listen to four speakers. Which question above does each person answer?

Speaker 1: ___   Speaker 3: ___

Speaker 2: ___   Speaker 4: ___

C Listen again and answer the questions.

Speaker 1

1 What age does the speaker think is best?

2 What three factors are important?

Speaker 2

3 What does the speaker think the minimum and maximum age should be?

4 What two factors need to be balanced?

Speaker 3

5 Why do you need to understand yourself and your relationship?

6 What is the wrong age, according to the speaker?

Speaker 4

7 When does the speaker think it's OK for a young person to make a choice?

8 What advice does the speaker give to other people?

D Match the phrases in bold with the meanings a)–e).

1 I don't think there's any **hard and fast** rule.

2 She's **still going strong** now she's over seventy.

3 You have to **strike a balance** between maturity and energy.

4 It **has to do with** giving yourself enough time to get to know yourself.

5 That **worked for** me.

a) was successful

b) choose a moderate way, compromise

c) fixed, definite

d) is connected to

e) continuing to be successful

VOCABULARY *PLUS* word formation

5A Complete the text with the correct form of the words in capitals.

Motivating students	
Students are motivated to learn by a variety of factors. Some look for a sense of personal 1_____ while others enjoy being 2_____ as a member of a learning group.	ACHIEVE INVOLVEMENT
Teachers sometimes make the mistake of over-praising students. It is better to show honest 3_____ rather than a mechanical or exaggerated response. If a student makes a mistake, 4_____ responding by using expressions such as 'I understand why you say that, but ...'. Your aim should be to 5_____ students to take risks and not to fear that they will be 6_____ for getting something wrong.	APPRECIATE PRACTICAL COURAGE JUDGEMENT
A teacher also needs to be seen to be fair and not show any 7_____ for one student over another. A lesson should be a 8_____ encounter for every student in the class.	PREFER SATISFY
However, always remember that some factors are outside your control. For example a student's worries about a family issue may be 9_____ with his or her concentration. In this situation, the best 10_____ is to give students the opportunity to contribute but not to force them if they don't want to.	INTERFERENCE ADVISOR

B Put the words in the correct group according to the pronunciation of the underlined letter(s).

| appr<u>e</u>ciate   obl<u>i</u>ge   <u>e</u>njoy   pr<u>e</u>tence |
| ach<u>ie</u>vement   pr<u>e</u>fer   pr<u>e</u>ference   adv<u>i</u>se |
| <u>e</u>ncourage |

/ɪ/   l<u>i</u>ttle

/iː/   <u>ea</u>t

/aɪ/   sk<u>y</u>

/e/   r<u>e</u>d

C ▶ 6.2 Listen and check. Then listen and repeat.

2020 VISION

The iPhone will be a distant memory and England's footballers will have had two more failed attempts at winning the World Cup. But what will a day in your life be like in 2020? Luis Villazon lets you peer into the future …

06.45

The alarm clock goes off. It's set for 07.00, but the clock's connected to the internet and has woken you fifteen minutes earlier than usual because the traffic reports from www.mycommute.com are predicting longer delays today due to a Tube strike. The internet radio station streams music from a standardised station playlist. But the HomeDJ service means that the news, traffic and weather are local, and are customised for you using the preferences that you set on their website. 1___

07.15

Breakfast is toast, plus an apple that's been stored in a FrootStore bag. This is a plastic bag you can buy from a supermarket that's impregnated with a compound that inhibits ethylene – the naturally produced gas compound that encourages fruit to ripen. 2___

07.50

Your journey to work is still by car – the public transport infrastructure hasn't improved much during the last ten years. It's now almost impossible to buy a new car that isn't at least a hybrid, uses regenerative braking (which charges a battery as you brake) and smart idling (which cuts the engine if you stop for more than a few seconds). Service stations now have fast-charge points at some locations where you can leave your car recharging while you have a coffee.

18.30

All the checkouts at your local supermarket are self-service. 3___ Most food manufacturers now label their products with food miles and some have gone a step further with a 'carbon foodprint' – the total carbon emitted during the production process, not just transportation.

18.45

Dinner is Bosnian meatballs with 'Kljukuša' (a sort of baked hash brown) because favourite TV cook Jamie Oliver – now in his mid-40s – is touring Central Europe for his latest video podcast series. Several broadcasters now transmit programmes simultaneously through the aerial and over the internet. Commercial TV revenues continue to slide. 4___

19.30

While you eat dinner, you check your LifeSaver account. This contains all the audio and video you uploaded at a few points during the day, recorded by a tiny camera built into your glasses. LifeSaver picks out the most significant moments and sends out a video stream to everyone who has signed up to receive them.

23.30

Through the night, while you're asleep and electricity demand is low, wind and wave power continue to supply electricity to the national grid. Combined with the photovoltaic cells that you put on the roof three years ago, more than fifteen per cent of your total electricity now comes from green sources. 5___ The smart meter allows you to keep track of your electricity consumption.

READING

1A Read the article. Which of the following topics are not mentioned?

work	food
transport	shopping
clothes	social networking
relationships	newspapers
energy	radio and television

B Five sentences have been removed from the article. Choose from sentences a)–f) the one which fits each gap (1–5). There is one sentence you do not need to use.

a) This is apart from a single 'assisted checkout', intended for customers with disabilities and staffed on demand.

b) Long showers and keeping the TV on standby are things of the past.

c) But if you buy one every time you feel tired, it soon adds up.

d) Fewer people are prepared to sit through live adverts now.

e) It holds everything from your apples to avocados in their pre-ripe condition until the time you want to eat them.

f) The info is dropped seamlessly into the programme between songs.

C Read the article again. Are the statements true (T), false (F) or is the information not given (NG)?

1 You are woken up early because of an important news bulletin.

2 The music on the radio is personalised according to your preferences.

3 You can buy fruit pre-packaged in a FrootStore bag.

4 Almost all new cars on the road are designed to conserve energy.

5 In many supermarkets you can judge for yourself how much carbon has been used in the production of particular food.

6 You can get daily recipes on TV.

7 You can't decide which video moments are sent out by LifeSaver.

8 Your own home contributes fifteen per cent of the electricity you use.

GRAMMAR future perfect and continuous

2 Underline the correct alternative.

1 Nine o'clock's too late to arrive. The concert *will start/will be starting/will have started* by then.

2 You can use my desk. I *won't use/won't be using/won't have used* it tomorrow as I'm away.

3 Professor Sawali will be happy to lead a discussion during the conference as she *'ll attend/'ll be attending/'ll have attended* it anyway.

4 Will you still *need/be needing/have needed* me when I'm sixty-four?

5 The well-known author *will sign/will be signing/will have signed* copies of his book between ten and noon on Wednesday.

6 Your two-day visit *will involve/will be involving/will have involved* a factory tour and several meetings.

7 We're planning a series of programmes which *will consist/will be consisting/will have consisted* of interviews interspersed with film footage.

8 By this time tomorrow the championship draw *will happen/will be happening/will have happened* and we'll know who we're playing.

3A Complete the predictions made in the 1950s about life in 2020. Use the future perfect or future continuous. If neither are possible, use the future simple.

1 The world / experience / mini ice-age / at that time.

The world will be experiencing a mini ice-age at that time.

2 The average weight / adult male / go down / to seventy kilos.

_____

3 Smoking / ban / completely / in all public areas.

_____

4 Every city / own / a big computer.

_____

5 Everyone / drive / flying cars.

_____

6 Men and women / wear / same clothes.

_____

7 Poverty and famine / halve.

_____

8 Every company / belong / its workers.

_____

B Which predictions above have already come true (✓), which may well come true (?) and which are unlikely to come true (✗)?

VOCABULARY optimism/pessimism

4 Write letters to complete the words.

1 pessimistic = glo <u>o</u> <u>m</u> y

2 good and bad experiences = u__ __ __ __ __ __ __ __ __ __

3 hopeful = pr__ __ __ __ __ __ __

4 emotions which are neither positive nor negative = m__ __ __ __ f__ __ __ __ __ __ __

5 see the positive side of things = __ __ __ __ __ __ __ __ __ __ __ __ __ __ __ side

6 move in a good direction = take one step __ __ __ __ __ __ __ __

7 positive = up__ __ __ __

8 fear = dr__ __ __ __

9 hopelessness = de__ __ __ __ __ __

10 give the feeling that things will be good = fill w__ __ __ op__ __ __ __ __ __

WRITING a letter; linkers of purpose

5A Complete the sentences with the linkers in the box.

| for in order to   because   not to   so that   so as not to |

1 You shouldn't keep quiet just _____ you might hurt someone's feelings.

2 Make time to discuss your future roles now _____ experience problems later.

3 You should sit down together _____ a long chat about why you feel ashamed.

4 It sounds as if you need professional help _____ identify the reason for this secrecy.

5 Tell her how you feel _____ she leaves you alone.

6 Speak to her, _____ criticise her, but to find out why she does everything for him.

B Match the advice in sentences 1–6 above with problems a)–c).

a) My fiancé's mother still does all his washing, cooking and cleaning. We're getting married next month and I'm worried about his expectations. I have a full-time career.

b) I recently lost my temper and quit my job. The thing is I can't bear to tell my friends and family so I've asked my wife to keep it a secret. She thinks I'm stupid. What can I do?

c) I'm in a tutor group of two at college. My fellow student and I have little in common but she's always suggesting we do things socially. How can I get rid of her without offending her?

C Write a letter for a magazine (80–100 words) answering one of the problems above with your own ideas. Include at least two linkers of purpose.

VOCABULARY collocations

1A Complete the questions with the correct collocations.

1 How long have you had your current cr_____ ca_____?
2 Do you mind st_____ home al_____?
3 Have you ever ri_____ a sc_____? If not, would you like to?
4 Do you think it's OK for men to we___ make-up?
5 How la___ do you think parents should let children st_____ up?
6 Have you ever ru_____ your own bu_____? If not, would you enjoy it?
7 How many mobile phones have you ow_____?
8 How many so_____ ne_____ websites have you used, if any?
9 Have you ever done a pa_____-ti_____ job?
10 Would you feel safe tr_____ so_____ around another country?
11 When you were younger did you ever ba_____ for a toddler?
12 Should children get their ears pi_____?

B Answer each question using no more than three words.

FUNCTION persuading

2A Correct the mistakes in A's sentences.

1 **A:** Look at this picture. Isn't that it time that they banned 'size zero' models?

B: Well, clothes do look quite good on them.

A: Don't it matter to you that young girls think it's normal to be so skinny?

B: I've never really thought about it much.

A: Well you should. It's not clearly right.

B: Yeah, I'm sure you're right.

2 **A:** Aren't you thinking that they should use technology in football games?

B: What, you mean instead of referees?

A: Yeah, to make decisions. No one can't see it would be fairer.

B: But you need referees for all sorts of reasons.

A: Yeah, but sure it's more important that decisions are correct.

B: Hmm. I suppose you have a point.

B ▶ 6.3 Listen and mark the main stresses in A's sentences.

C Listen again and say A's sentences at the same time. Pay attention to stress and intonation.

LEARN TO ask for clarification

3A Put the phrases in bold in the correct order.

1 **A:** Do you like me in this dress?

B: I prefer the white one.

A: **you / is / so / saying / that / what / 're** this one, which cost a fortune, looks terrible.

_____

B: No, I mean the white one makes you look slimmer.

A: **look / so / fat / other / I / in / words!**

_____

B: No, no, you're twisting my words. I just meant that you look *even* slimmer in the white one.

2 **A:** Don't you think we should pay a decorator to do it?

B: **is / you / getting / 're / at / what** you don't think I can do it.

_____

A: I didn't mean that. It's just that it might be quicker and save us money.

B: **that / your / so / gather / is / point / I** I might mess it up.

_____

A: No, but you're a perfectionist and you know how long it takes you to do things.

B: **I / right / got / it / 've / if / so,** you'd rather spend money and end up with a worse job!

_____

A: Not exactly …

B ▶ 6.4 Listen and check.

GRAMMAR future perfect and continuous

1 Complete the articles with the future perfect or continuous form of an appropriate verb. If neither are possible, use the future simple.

By 2025

By 2025 in many countries the number of people over sixty-five [1]_____ and far fewer people of working age [2]_____ taxes to support them. It is almost certainly the case that many older people [3]_____ enough for their old age and [4]_____ an uncertain future or one of poverty. Experts from many different countries [5]_____ the issue in ???????? ??? ??? course of the next week.

> not save
> discuss
> pay
> face
> double

By 2050

Sixty per cent of humanity [6]_____ in cities. They [7]_____ petrol or diesel cars. All cars [8]_____ hybrid engines so that they run on electricity as well as a more traditional fuel. Robots [9]_____ humans in all boring, mundane jobs and as a result, people [10]_____ in more stimulating jobs but with fewer hours.

> work
> have
> replace
> drive
> live

GRAMMAR articles

2 Add *a(n)* or *the* in ten places in the text.

If you want to win at sports, choose red shirt. Research by two scientists from University of Durham shows that team's chance of winning is influenced by colour of their shirts. As part of their investigation, scientists examined football results since end of Second World War and found clear connection between wearing red and winning. Teams who wore orange or yellow shirt had worst records.

VOCABULARY review

3 Complete the sentences with the correct word/ phrase.

1 influence/promote

a) There's a meeting in June to _____ trade between Scotland and Thailand.

b) It's impossible to _____ the lottery results.

2 commercials/campaigns

a) I hate it when they put on _____ straight after the opening titles of a programme.

b) The best advertising _____ use a variety of media: posters, TV, videos.

3 damaged/distorted

a) The press _____ what I said. I never said she was violent, just that she had a bad temper.

b) The reports about his behaviour _____ his reputation badly.

4 enhance/have a beneficial effect

a) These high-quality 3D glasses will _____ your viewing experience.

b) Owning a pet has been shown to _____ on health. Pet owners attend the doctor's surgery less often than people without pets.

5 elderly/mature

a) Please give up this seat for the _____ or disabled.

b) Many trees only start producing fruit when they are _____.

6 come of age/act his age

a) Look at him dancing. I wish he'd _____ more.

b) When does a boy _____ in the tribe?

7 obscure/unrealistic

a) For some _____ reason, James won't tell me why he turned down the job.

b) Sonia had _____ ambitions to become a singer. Her singing was only very ordinary.

8 weird/dreadful

a) I had a _____ dream last night. I dreamt I'd won a million dollars and I'd bought myself a boat.

b) We went for a picnic yesterday but the weather was _____ and we had to come home.

4A Look at the underlined sounds in each group. Circle the word with the different sound.

1 dam<u>a</u>ge, prom<u>i</u>sing, advert<u>i</u>se
2 benefi<u>c</u>ial, a<u>ch</u>ieve, revolut<u>i</u>onise
3 <u>a</u>mbitious, predict<u>a</u>ble, m<u>a</u>turity
4 w<u>ea</u>r, w<u>ei</u>rd, interf<u>e</u>rence
5 dr<u>ea</u>dful, pret<u>e</u>nd, appr<u>e</u>ciate
6 camp<u>ai</u>gn, r<u>ea</u>ction, br<u>ea</u>kthrough

B ▶ RC3.1 **Listen and check. Then listen and repeat.**

FUNCTION suggesting ideas

5 Underline the correct alternative.

A: Can we brainstorm ideas for Jack's leaving present?

B: Could we go ¹*for/towards* a gadget of some kind?

C: ²*What/How* do you think about something to do with cars?

D: I was ³*wondering/thinking* of something similar. For instance, it ⁴*will/would* be great to buy him a ticket to a Formula-1 race.

A: Would you ⁵*consider/strike* something completely ⁶*predictable/different*? Suppose we ⁷*get/should get* him a place on a course?

B: What kind of course?

A: Well, how do flying lessons ⁸*please/strike* you?

B: I think we're on the wrong ⁹*line/track* here. How do you ¹⁰*feel/think* about a book on cars?

C: It doesn't ¹¹*strike/grab* me. It's not ¹²*obscure/original* enough.

D: I agree. I'm ¹³*torn/tearing* between the Formula-1 ticket and the flying lessons.

A: Shall we vote? OK, the Formula-1 ticket wins. So let's ¹⁴*go/do* with that.

VOCABULARY optimism/pessimism

6 Complete the underlined phrases.

A: So, how are you getting on with the course?

B: ¹<u>I / mix / feeling / it</u>. I'm finding the module on statistics very difficult. It feels like I'm ²<u>take / step / forward / two / back</u> but I'm enjoying the other modules.

A: That's not surprising. Everyone ³<u>have / their / up / down</u> when they start university.

B: Yeah, but ⁴<u>I / dread</u> the exams.

A: Nobody ⁵<u>look / forward / take / exams</u> but I'm sure you'll do fine. ⁶<u>Look / bright / side</u>. This time next month, they'll all be over.

1 *I have mixed feelings about it* _____
2 _____
3 _____
4 _____
5 _____
6 _____

VOCABULARY *PLUS* compound nouns

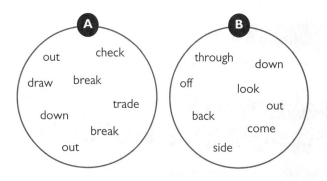

A
out
check
draw
break
down
trade
break
out

B
through
down
off
look
out
back
come
side

7A Join a word from A with one from B to complete sentences 1–8.

1 Its discovery made cooking possible and was a _____ in human evolution.

2 As more and more of us get our news online, the _____ for their survival is poor.

3 It can be hard to read, but the main _____ is that it's yet another gadget to carry around.

4 This is the best solution when there is a complete _____ in a marriage.

5 People stayed up to hear the _____ and to find out who would be the next president.

6 There are lots of positives, and the only _____ is that you have to take it for a walk, even in the rain.

7 Most people use these instead of cash when they pay at a supermarket __ _____.

8 When people are choosing one, there's always a _____ between speed and safety.

B What is being talked about in sentences 1–8 above?

GRAMMAR modal verbs and phrases

8 Complete the conversations with a modal verb or phrase.

A: Did you do the whole walk?

B: We ¹_____ climb to the top but we ²_____ stay long because of the weather.

A: Were you ³_____ see much of the view?

A: You really ⁴_____ to fly when you've got such bad flu.

B: But if I don't get on that plane I ⁵_____ to go to the wedding.

A: But when you try to check in, they might not ⁶_____ fly. The rules are quite strict.

A: What time do your parents say you ⁷_____ go to bed?

B: I'm ⁸_____ be in bed by ten but I often stay up till eleven. What about you?

A: I'm ⁹_____ stay up till ten at the weekend but my parents ¹⁰_____ me go to bed at nine during the week.

GRAMMAR conditionals

9 Underline the correct alternative.

PRICE WARS – WHO'S THE VICTIM?

If you ¹*own/owned* a shop and you ²*wanted/would want* to sell a product, you might put it on sale, but if you ³*would/were* to lower the price, you'd make less profit. However, if you keep the price the same but ⁴*would call/ call* it a 'sale price', customers ⁵*will/would* feel they're getting a bargain. Some other tricks are:

- **Ninety-nining** – If the price ⁶*is/were* £15.99, it seems like 15-something. If the same product were priced at £16.00, it ⁷*doesn't/wouldn't* sell as well.

- **Buy one, get one free** – If you ⁸*buy/bought* two items, the less expensive one is 'free'. In fact, ⁹*provided/supposing* the shop is not losing money, you ¹⁰*can/could* be sure that the profit is included in the price of the more expensive item. ¹¹*Unless/ Provided* you really need two items, you end up buying more than you planned.

- **Baiting** – This is when an already cheap product is offered even cheaper. ¹²*Unless/If* you're not very disciplined, once you get into the shop you'll buy other things.

VOCABULARY PLUS word formation

10A Find ten verbs in the word square.

E	N	C	O	U	R	A	G	E
Z	I	I	A	P	S	D	H	H
X	N	N	P	R	E	V	M	E
I	T	V	P	E	B	I	C	V
M	E	O	R	F	K	S	I	Z
P	R	L	E	E	V	E	K	S
R	F	V	C	R	S	S	F	V
E	E	E	I	J	U	D	G	E
S	R	S	A	T	I	S	F	Y
S	E	M	T	R	E	A	C	T
H	B	Z	E	N	J	W	H	H

B Complete the questions with the noun form of eight of the verbs above.

1 How can we show our _____ for everything she has done for us?

2 What are your first _____ of the new building?

3 What's the best _____ you've ever been given?

4 How can we measure customer _____ with the product?

5 What's your _____ to the news about your ex-wife?

6 Who gave you the most _____ to succeed when you were younger?

7 How often do you experience _____ on your radio?

8 What's your _____ as regards colour? Blue or yellow?

FUNCTION persuading

11 Complete the conversation with the words in the box. You do not need to use three words.

shouldn't	surely	doesn't	wouldn't	haven't
aren't	clearly	don't	isn't	

A: Tom, ¹_____ you think we should start packing?

B: ²_____ it won't take all night to pack. We don't leave till noon.

A: ³_____ we at least begin? Last time it took ages – ⁴_____ we didn't allow enough time then.

B: Only because I couldn't find my glasses!

A: Exactly. So ⁵_____ it better to do it now to give ourselves plenty of time?

B: You could start. I'll just throw in a few things later.

A: But ⁶_____ it be quicker if we did it together?

TEST

Circle the correct option to complete the sentences.

1 I have the _____ that he's not what he seems.

   a) judgement   b) pretence   c) impression

2 Before the invention of _____ people paid for everything in cash.

   a) the credit card   b) a credit card
   c) the credit cards

3 The designers have come up with a new _____ for the company. It looks like a parachute.

   a) slogan   b) jingle   c) logo

4 She _____ her first business when she was only eighteen.

   a) made   b) took   c) ran

5 There will be a bonus paid to all managers _____ they meet their targets.

   a) unless   b) provided   c) as long

6 Did you _____ much?

   a) practise   b) practice   c) practical

7 I think we're _____ the wrong track here.

   a) in   b) on   c) along

8 The _____ for next year's harvests is very poor and a widespread famine is predicted.

   a) outlook   b) outcome   c) downside

9 Children under thirteen _____ join social networking sites but they often do.

   a) aren't supposed to   b) don't have to
   c) aren't allowed

10 Are you allowed to _____ make-up at school?

   a) put   b) get   c) wear

11 Don't phone me until the afternoon. I _____ to our Washington office by then.

   a) 'll be speaking   b) 'll speak   c) 'll have spoken

12 She seems very keen and competent and has _____ plans for the future of the club.

   a) weird   b) predictable   c) ambitious

13 _____ your headphones today? I've broken mine.

   a) Will you be using   b) Will you use
   c) Will you have used

14 A third runway has been approved at the airport. What _____ for local residents over the next few years?

   a) will that be meaning   b) will that mean
   c) will that have meant

15 _____ buy the property we would need to charge a high rent.

   a) If we will   b) Unless we   c) If we were to

16 _____ unfair that wealthy people pay a smaller proportion of taxes than those with less money?

   a) Don't you think   b) Isn't
   c) Doesn't it seem

17 So _____ that no-one knows the answer, they're just guessing?

   a) what you're saying is   b) what you're getting is
   c) in other kinds of words

18 Contact lenses _____ eyecare in the mid-twentieth century.

   a) had a detrimental effect   b) revolutionised
   c) altered

19 The product has been _____ by leading medical experts.

   a) endorsed   b) influenced   c) branded

20 The whole feel of the website is very _____ and positive.

   a) upbeat   b) cynical   c) promise

21 The book is about an _____ sect or religion which existed in the fourteenth century.

   a) absurd   b) obscure   c) unrealistic

22 At school they _____ three hours homework a night.

   a) let us do   b) made us do   c) allowed us to do

23 There was a _____ in the talks at the very last minute and an agreement has been reached.

   a) breakdown   b) breakthrough   c) trade-off

24 He won't play in the World Cup _____ completely fit.

   a) unless he's   b) if he's   c) until he'll be

25 He's amazing. He looks really _____.

   a) his prime   b) young for his age   c) immature

26 Would you consider _____ a consultant?

   a) hiring   b) hire   c) to hire

27 If I get high enough grades I'll start _____ next September.

   a) the university   b) university   c) a university

28 The rise of drug abuse fills me with _____.

   a) optimism   b) despair   c) gloomy

29 Last Tuesday for the first time scientists _____ communicate with a patient in a deep coma.

   a) could   b) were able   c) managed to

30 _____ is like jam – you can't spread even a little without getting some on yourself!

   a) The happiness   b) A happiness   c) Happiness

TEST RESULT /30

VOCABULARY television

1 Complete the crossword with types of TV programme.

Across

1 A _____ affairs programme covers up-to-date social and political stories.

4 A _____ opera has romance and drama and is on regularly.

7 Number 8 down is one kind of _____ show.

9 This programme features animals.

10 A set of programmes, e.g., a new _____ of *Top Gear*.

13 A programme about something real.

14 This programme mixes reality and fiction.

Down

1 Actors wear clothes from the past in a _____ drama.

2 It's full of suspense.

3 This type of show often puts ordinary people in extraordinary situations.

5 A private eye solves a murder every week in a _____ series.

6 Find out what happened today on the _____.

8 Competitors answer questions on a _____ show.

10 This has the same characters each week in funny situations.

11 Short funny pieces are acted out on a _____ show.

12 It's a story or drama broadcast in different parts.

GRAMMAR quantifiers

2 Cross out the incorrect alternative in each sentence.

1 He's got *quite a few/many/little* English-speaking friends.

2 *Several/Every/Each* room has a whiteboard.

3 We have *a little/a small amount of/little* money left, so we can afford a coffee.

4 *Much/A small number of/A great deal of* time was spent explaining the error.

5 I'll buy *either of/all of/both of* them, I like them so much.

6 *A few/A little/Several* books are missing from the library.

7 I've got *no/any/some* idea what to do if the car breaks down.

8 I can't see *any/many/no* reasons for sleeping here tonight.

3 Complete the report with the quantifiers in the box.

hardly any	both	a large number
a few	no	quite a few	all	any
each	a large amount		

WHAT'S YOUR MEDIUM?

We asked you how you prefer to get information: via the internet, TV, radio, or newspapers/magazines? Here are the results.

Internet: 67%

Unsurprisingly, a majority of people said that the internet is their primary source of information, and in fact ¹_____ respondents, only about 2%, said they never used it. Two main advantages of the internet were mentioned by ²_____ people, indeed by most of them: easy access and up-to-date content. ³_____ of these features were given as problems with newspapers and magazines.

TV: 21%

Surprisingly, ⁴_____ of respondents, more than 94%, say they spend more time watching TV than they used to although about a quarter of TV viewing is done through the internet. Both normal and internet-based TV remain important sources of information, and ⁵_____ of them has maintained healthy audience figures.

Radio: 7%

Just as internet TV has been a boost to that medium, the internet has helped radio maintain its status as a preferred source of information for at least ⁶_____ respondents who spend ⁷_____ of time listening to their radios.

Newspapers/Magazines: 5%

Most respondents commented that although newspapers or magazines were more reliable than ⁸_____ the electronic sources, in fact ⁹_____ of the three, TV, radio and the internet, was more convenient. Four people said that they use ¹⁰_____ other source but newspapers and magazines.

LISTENING

4A ▶ **7.1 Listen to four people talk about their favourite childhood TV programme and complete the table.**

Speaker	Programme name	Programme type
1		
2		
3		
4		

B Listen again. Which speaker (1–4) thinks:

a) Kids learnt how to make things.

b) It was something kids understood better than their parents.

c) Every episode took kids on a journey.

d) If you made an effort you could win a prize.

e) Kids learnt a lot that helped them with growing up.

f) Kids enjoyed the unconventional nature of it.

g) It involved a strong element of fantasy.

h) It was very realistic and right for the age group.

C Match the words in bold with meanings a)–f).

1 He's then transported to a world that **corresponds with** the outfit that he's wearing.

2 It's hard to underestimate its cultural **impact**.

3 It kind of **bridges the gap** between the two.

4 It deals with issues … in an **unpatronising, uncondescending** way.

5 One sketch would **morph** into another.

6 We'd spend our entire lunch break … remembering all the **catchphrases**.

a) expressions which are linked to a performer or programme and are very recognisable

b) appropriately intelligent

c) matches

d) connects

e) influence or effect

f) change

VOCABULARY *PLUS* multi-word verbs

5A Complete the sentences with the words in the box.

into   across   out (x3)   up   down   back

1 If I say something offensive, I'm often too stubborn to take it _____.

2 I can put _____ with a noisy hotel room more than a dirty one.

3 If someone's car breaks _____, I know how to fix it.

4 Hard work brings _____ the best in me.

5 I come _____ as being more sociable than I really am.

6 If it turned _____ that my partner had lied to me, I would be disappointed in him.

7 If I locked my keys in my car, I would simply break _____ it.

8 When I agree to do something, I never pull _____ even if I feel ill.

B ▶ **7.2 Listen to the sentences above and underline the stressed part of the multi-word verb. Then listen and repeat.**

C Complete the sentences with a multi-word verb from Exercise 5A but with a different or slightly different meaning.

1 I'm good in situations where communications have _____ _____ and people refuse to talk to each other.

2 I always buy a new version of a product as soon as it is _____ _____.

3 If I saw a bus _____ _____, I would try to stop it and get on rather than wait for the next one.

4 Smells rather than images _____ me _____ to my childhood.

5 If a homeless person knocked on my door in the middle of winter, I would _____ them _____ for the night.

6 If I _____ _____ a large amount of money in the street, I would hand it into the police.

7 When a lot of people _____ _____ for a political demonstration, I'm usually not one of them.

8 If I needed a job, I would rather work in a field that I know than try to _____ _____ a new area.

D Tick the sentences in Exercises 5A and C that are true for you.

READING

SAY 'CHEESE' NOW ... SUE LATER

The McGraw family of Dublin expected their visit to Poland to be full of adventure and surprises. But they never expected to find themselves four metres high, beaming at the world from the wall of an underground station.

'We turned a corner onto the platform, and there we were in living colour,' said Paul McGraw. 'It was a family photo that I'd posted on our family blog last year but in the middle of an advertisement for an electronics appliance chain. No one ever asked us for permission,' added McGraw. 'Someone obviously downloaded it off our blog.' [1]___

The unauthorised use of photographs downloaded from internet photo albums is not uncommon, and it would be impossible to count how many local advertising agencies have avoided costly photography and copyright fees by simply downloading material they find on the internet.

'It's simply too tempting for them,' said advertising lawyer Lee Szymanski. 'In most cases, where the advertisement is going to appear in a small geographical area, the chances of getting caught are almost zero. [2]___ And if they do get caught, the legal process is too complicated, expensive, and frankly unclear for it to be worth pursuing.'

As rarely as the culprits are caught, there are countless known cases of such 'borrowing'. In one case, a major mobile phone provider used photographs taken from an internet photo album site in one of its campaigns, and justified it by saying that it was promoting creative freedom'. [3]___

Professional photographers have also been affected, and the law has not been clear in deciding if unauthorised use is legal or not. A California newspaper used a copyrighted photo taken by a professional photographer without seeking his permission, and when he sued them, the jury decided it was a case of 'fair use' – leaving the photographer with nothing but legal fees and frustration. On the other hand, a New York judge awarded a Quebec-based photographer over $60,000 in damages when he sued an online travel agency for their use of four photos he had shot in Ghana. Meanwhile, the photos had been duplicated and used on at least 200 other websites, according to the photographer. [4]___

'Professional photographers are in a better position to seek damages because they copyright their work,' said Szymanski. 'But for most people who simply upload snapshots to share with friends, there's very little they can do.'

So the next time you upload a photo of yourself with a big grin, don't be surprised if you find yourself advertising toothpaste somewhere in the world. [5]___

1A Read the article about unauthorised use of photos. Which of the following are mentioned as using photographs without permission?

a newspaper

a telephone company

a social networking website

a city transport company

a travel agency

a professional photographer

an electronics shop

B Five sentences have been removed from the article. Choose from sentences a)–f) the one which fits each gap (1–5). There is one sentence you do not need to use.

a) 'The value of my work drops every time someone uses it without paying,' he said. 'I can't describe the anger I feel.'

b) Who in the UK would ever find out that their image appears in a billboard advert somewhere in New Zealand?

c) 'We think that amateur photographers should be happy for their work to gain so much exposure,' said a company representative.

d) Or furniture. Or electronic appliances. Or cars ...

e) 'In fact it didn't really bother us,' he added. 'But I can imagine someone else being very upset.'

f) There are cases where the courts have not looked favourably upon the photographer's claim.

GRAMMAR reported speech

2 Underline the correct alternative.

THE **WORST** INTERVIEW I EVER HAD
– BY ACTOR RUDY SEARS

It was with a young journalist, and he started out by asking me normal questions. He asked how long it [1]*took/had taken* me to become successful as an actor, and I told him that I [2]*didn't remember/hadn't remembered* a particular point where I could say I was successful. He asked who [3]*did have/had had* the greatest influence on my acting style, and I said that my mother [4]*has/had* – she was an amateur actress. Then he started on the personal questions: he asked if my marriage [5]*was breaking down/broke down* and if it was true that my wife [6]*wanted/wants* a divorce. I said I [7]*won't/wouldn't* discuss that and that I [8]*must/had to* go. In the end he wrote a very negative article about me, but it actually helped my career.

3 Change the sentences to reported speech.

A: Why did you come here today?

1 He wanted to know _____.

B: I've been trying to see you since yesterday.

2 I said that _____.

A: Please close the door and have a seat.

3 He asked _____.

A: How can I help you?

4 He enquired _____.

B: I have information that Mario the Snitch will be killed tomorrow.

5 I told _____.

A: What makes you think this might happen?

6 He wanted to know _____.

B: Don't waste time asking me questions.

7 I told him _____.

A: Shall I let the cops know?

8 He asked _____ and I told him it was up to him.

VOCABULARY reporting verbs

4A Complete the interviewer's questions (1–6) and the answers a)–f) with the correct forms of the verbs.

Have you ever …

1 been persuaded _____ (take part) in a film you didn't want to?

2 threatened _____ (walk out) of a film?

3 suggested _____ (make) changes to a film?

4 been accused _____ (lie)?

5 apologised _____ (do) something when you didn't mean it?

6 admitted _____ (do) something that you didn't do?

a) No, but sometimes I've refused _____ (say) 'sorry'.

b) Not usually, but once I insisted _____ (change) my script in a key scene.

c) No, but I've done the opposite: denied _____ (do) something that I *did do*.

d) No, once I've agreed _____ (take on) a job, I would never leave halfway through.

e) No, not even when they've offered _____ (pay) me a fortune.

f) No, I always try _____ (be) honest.

B Match questions 1–6 with answers a)–f).

WRITING a discursive essay; linkers of contrast

5A Look at the sentences from an essay on the topic below. Are they for (✓) or against (✗) the topic?

Topic: Most information on the internet is unreliable.

1 Most internet writers are amateurs, but many give objective information.

2 The internet is a convenient source of information, but its accessibility can also mean that this information is not trustworthy.

3 Of course there's some inaccurate content, but it's the reader's responsibility to identify the reliable information.

4 Wiki contributors try to give accurate information but too many don't use reliable sources.

5 Many amateur news websites look serious, but that doesn't make them accurate.

6 These weaknesses exist, but there are reasons to trust much internet content as well.

B Rewrite each sentence above with the linker given. Pay attention to punctuation.

1 (although) _____

2 (while) _____

3 (however) _____

4 (despite) _____

5 (although) _____

6 (while) _____

VOCABULARY the press

1A Add vowels to make words.

1 s _ ppl _ m _ nt
2 c _ rc _ l _ t _ _ n
3 r _ _ d _ rsh _ p
4 br _ _ dsh _ _ t
5 s _ ns _ t _ _ n _ l _ sm

6 c _ l _ mn _ sts
7 b _ _ s _ d
8 _ d _ t _ r _ _ l
9 f _ _ t _ r _
10 t _ bl _ _ d

B Complete the letter with the words above.

To the Editor,
I am writing to complain about recent changes to your newspaper. I believe I am typical of the paper's 1_____ in that I am an ordinary working person, and I strongly object to the 2_____ of some of your recent headlines and stories, which does not suit a serious 3_____ newspaper like yours. This style of reporting and the new colour 4_____ are more typical of 5_____ newspapers. Also, the recent 6_____ article on the public transport system was full of the reporter's own opinion and was very 7_____ . I think you should save your opinions for the 8_____ page as that's what it is for, or let one of your 9_____ state the paper's position in their daily column.

   I am sure the reason for these changes was to increase 10_____, but it has made me decide to cancel my subscription.

FUNCTION adding emphasis

2 Rewrite the sentences using one of the emphasising structures: pronoun/noun + be + *the one who* or *the* + adjective + *thing is*.

1 He's always complaining, not me.
   He's the one who's always complaining, not me.

2 You were asking about the price.
   _____

3 The photo is incredible because of the light.
   _____

4 The fact that people want to buy this paper is remarkable.
   _____

5 They want to have a big party, not us.
   _____

6 The number of adverts is ridiculous.
   _____

3A Correct the mistakes in the underlined parts of the conversation.

A: [1]This is total ridiculously. Where are my keys? [2]The thing is annoying that I had them a minute ago. Oh, [3]does it make me so mad when I can't find them!

B: Well, [4]you're one who's always telling me to put them somewhere safe. Have you tried the door?

A: [5]There isn't a way I'd leave them there!

B: OK, I'm just trying to help. [6]There's no need to get into such state!

A: I'm not 'in a state!' Now [7]where on earth I last had them?

B ▶ 7.3 Listen and circle the stressed words. Then listen and say the sentences at the same time.

LEARN TO make guesses

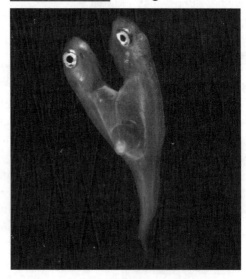

4A Put the words in the correct order.

1 it's / reckon / I / fish / Siamese / a
   I reckon it's a Siamese fish

2 it's / photo / hoax / a / surely
   _____

3 upstream / plant / perhaps / nuclear / a / there's
   _____

4 might / fish / be / it / two
   _____

5 imagine / it's / say / I'd / genuine / to / but / it's / hard
   _____

B Match sentence halves 1–5 above with a)–e).

a) ____ – why would anyone fake this?
b) ____ just like twins who are connected.
c) ____ and this is a genetic mutation.
d) ____ with one on top of the other.
e) ____ and someone's just playing a joke.

GRAMMAR conditionals

1A Read the articles and find the mistake in each picture.

EURO-MILLION DILEMMA

One morning in 2006, Jim Farley was outside a Dublin bank when five bundles of cash fell from a security van which was driving away. He took them home and kept them for two days before phoning the bank. He rang from a payphone in a terrible state of anxiety as he didn't know what to do. The security director persuaded him to hand in the money. It came to almost €1,000,000.

PARIS MÉTRO RESCUE

Jean LeBois was waiting for his métro train with his son, Roger, aged four. Suddenly, a man collapsed on the platform and then fell onto the tracks. A train was approaching and LeBois had to make a split-second decision whether to help. He leapt off the platform and pressed the man into the space between the tracks. Five carriages went overhead before the train stopped. Both men emerged safe to the applause of the onlookers.

B Read the articles again and complete the sentences.

1 If Jim _____ (not walk) by the bank that day, he _____ (not see) the money.

2 His call _____ (trace) if he _____ (phone) from a mobile.

3 If he _____ (not come forward) with the money, it's possible that the police _____ (never find) it.

4 He _____ (keep) the money if he _____ (not speak) to the security director.

5 Jim _____ (be) rich now if he _____ (keep) the money.

6 The man _____ (not fall) off the platform if he _____ (not collapse).

7 If the train _____ (stop), Jean _____ (not leap) onto the tracks.

8 The man _____ (be) dead now if Jean _____ (not jump) onto the tracks.

9 If the space _____ (not be) quite deep, both men _____ (kill) by the train.

10 If Jean _____ (have) more time to think, he probably _____ (not jump).

2 Complete the second sentence so that it has a similar meaning to the first. Use between two and five words including the word given.

1 I didn't know who he was so I didn't ask him for an autograph.
HIM
If I'd known who he was, I
_____ for an autograph.

2 You feel sick now because you ate too much.
SICK
You _____ if you had eaten less.

3 Anya's skis weren't very good and this could be the reason she didn't win the race.
MIGHT
Anya _____ if she'd had better skis.

4 The ambulance took a long time. Is that why they couldn't save him?
COULD
If the ambulance had got here sooner, _____ saved!

5 You're living in a one-bedroom flat today because you didn't take my advice.
LIVING
If you'd taken my advice, _____ in a one-bedroom flat today.

6 You weren't paying attention and so you didn't hear what I said.
IF
You would have heard what I said _____ attention.

7 Angie left the sat nav behind and we're lost.
LOST
We wouldn't _____ remembered the sat nav!

8 In my situation, what other choices were there?
YOU
What _____ if you'd been in my situation?

3A ▶ 8.1 Listen and write the phrases you hear.

1 _____
_____

2 _____
_____

3 _____
_____

B Listen again and mark the stressed words and any examples of weak forms with /əv/. Then listen and repeat.

LISTENING

4A You are going to listen to a lecture about an experiment to test people's behaviour. Look at the posters. What do you think the experiment was about?

B ▶ 8.2 Listen to Part 1 and check your ideas.

C Listen again. Complete the summary using no more than three words for each answer.

The lecture is about differences between people's behaviour when they ¹_____ and how they behave when they ²_____. It is in three parts:

First part: A description of ³_____ at Newcastle University.

Second part: What this tells us about ⁴_____ and behaviour.

Third part: A comparison with other key findings in the area.

The aim of the experiment was to discover whether the ⁵_____ that you are being watched can alter your behaviour. The scientists monitored ⁶_____ in a staff room to see how much people paid for their tea and coffee. Above it was a poster with the prices.

Each week they ⁷_____ on the poster. They found that people were ⁸_____ when they were watched by eyes than when there were pictures of flowers. They put ⁹_____ as much money in.

D ▶ 8.3 Listen to Part 2 and answer the questions.

1 Why is it important that our brains respond to faces and eyes?
2 How do people behave if they think they are being watched?
3 How did the researchers feel about the results?
4 How could a similar poster be used for speed cameras?
5 Where else could a poster be put?

VOCABULARY collocations

5 Use the clues to complete the puzzle. Then discover what you should do if you find it difficult to make decisions.

1	C								
2 G	A								
3 S					T				
4 C									
5 P				O					
6 P									
7 B									
8 F									
U									
9 A									
10 E									
11 W									
12 A									
D									

Clues

1 Sue's asked us to _____ the costs of the two designs before we choose one.
2 Lying to him will _____ all my principles. (2 words)
3 I've made a decision and I intend to _____ it. (2 words)
4 It took the two sides all day to _____ a decision. (2 words)
5 They can't _____ the decision any longer. We need an answer. (2 words)
6 The committee have agreed to _____ their decision until they have more facts.
7 Are you asking me to _____ all my beliefs?
8 You should _____ your ideals rather than chase fame and fortune.
9 When do you think the government will _____ a decision? (2 words)
10 We will have to _____ the proposal in detail.
11 He'll need to _____ the options before he makes a decision. (2 words)
12 We're trying to _____ what went wrong.

READING

1A Look at the picture. Which position do you usually sleep in?

A _____
B _____
C _____
D _____
E _____
F _____

...SLEEP POSITION GIVES PERSONALITY CLUE...

1 **You may already know if you function better in the morning or evening, but do you know what your sleep position can reveal?** Professor Chris Idzikowski, director of the Sleep Assessment and Advisory Service, has analysed six common sleeping positions and found that each is linked to a particular personality type. 'We are all aware of our body language when we are awake but this is the first time we have been able to see what our subconscious posture says about us. What's interesting is that the profile behind the posture is often very different from what we would expect.' These are the six positions studied by Professor Idzikowski:

2 ● **Starfish:** Lying on your back with both arms up around the pillow. These sleepers make good friends because they are always ready to listen to others, and offer help when needed. They generally don't like to be the centre of attention.

3 ● **Log:** Lying on your side with both arms down by your side. These sleepers are easy-going, social people who like being part of the in-crowd. They are trusting of strangers, in fact sometimes too trusting, to the point of being gullible.

4 ● **Freefaller:** Lying on your front with your hands around the pillow, and your head turned to one side. Often gregarious people who love to socialise, but can be nervy and become tense easily. They also can be thin-skinned underneath, and don't like criticism.

5 ● **Foetus:** Those who curl up in the foetus position are described as tough on the outside but sensitive at heart. They may be shy when they first meet somebody, but soon relax. More than twice as many women as men tend to adopt this position.

6 ● **Soldier:** Lying on your back with both arms pinned to your sides. People who sleep in this position are generally quiet and they don't like a fuss, but set themselves and others high standards.

7 ● **Yearner:** People who sleep on their side with both arms out in front are said to have an open nature, but can be suspicious, cynical and not believe anything they hear. They are slow to make up their minds, but once they have taken a decision, they are unlikely ever to change it.

B Read the article and write the name of each sleeping position under the correct picture.

C Which type of person are the following quotes about? Underline the part of the article which helped you decide.

1 'You don't like his shoes? Don't tell him, he'll blow up!'

2 'It takes a while to get to know him.'

3 'We threw a surprise party for him and he almost died of embarrassment.'

4 'No, you can't persuade him. He's decided what he wants.'

5 'Yeah, he wants everything to be perfect, so we're always working late.'

6 'He loves a good party and he's so laid back.'

D Find a word in the article which means:

1 physical position (paragraph 1)

2 a small group of people seen by others to be particularly popular or fashionable (paragraph 3)

3 ready to believe anything (paragraph 3)

4 someone who likes being with other people (paragraph 4)

5 too sensitive (paragraph 4)

6 anxious or excited behaviour often about unimportant things (paragraph 6)

VOCABULARY feelings

2 Rearrange the letters in bold to make words. The first letter is underlined.

1 It made me **necgir** when I realised how stupid I'd been. *cringe*

2 On that fine sunny day, Chris woke up feeling **gthrib** and **zyeber**.

3 Jane was at her **setowl beb** straight after the divorce.

4 It was 2 a.m. and I was still **ediw akewa** and completely **treal**.

5 The strange silence in the house gave me a **neess** of **dader**.

6 I **sisdepe** modern art with a **sanipso**.

7 He's often at his **streshap** when his team is in trouble.

8 Good news? You've got a real **cenobu** in your **pets**!

9 You decide which film to see. I'm not all that **sefsud**.

10 Sorry, I'm not really **no het lalb** today. I only slept three hours and feel a bit **gogyrg**.

GRAMMAR -ing form and infinitive

3A Underline the correct alternatives.

Scientists are learning more and more about sleeping and waking states. For example, did you know that ¹daydream/daydreaming can help you ²to solve/solving complex tasks? This is because it activates the part of the brain associated with ³tackle/tackling difficult problems. Also ⁴take/taking a nap in the middle of the day refreshes your brain. It's like ⁵to clear/clearing your email inbox so that there's room for new information. Interestingly, ⁶stay up/staying up all night, as many students do before exams, increases the ability to hold new facts by 40%. Some people don't seem ⁷to need/need much sleep. UK prime minister Margaret Thatcher was famous for ⁸be able/being able to run the country on just four hours sleep a night. However, the great scientist Albert Einstein tended ⁹require/to require ten hours a night, perhaps because he solved problems by ¹⁰sleep/sleeping on them.

B Which fact in the text above do you think is incorrect?

4 Complete the sentences with an -ing form or infinitive.

1 When / I / be / young, my father / teach / me / work hard / play hard.

   When I was young, my father taught me to work hard and play hard.

2 Jake / hate / not / able / play / football / because of his bad leg.

   _____

3 They / have / invite / Guido / give / talk / at / conference.

   _____

4 Olga / have / suggest / go for / picnic.

   _____

5 What / you / want / me / do?

   _____

6 Would / you / mind / tell / us / how old / you / be?

   _____

7 The firm / not / expect / have to / pay / the damage.

   _____

8 Can / I / persuade / you / change / your / mind?

   _____

9 It / be / not / worth / wait / any longer.

   _____

VOCABULARY PLUS idioms

5 Replace the underlined words with a phrase/idiom using the words in brackets.

   time after time

1 I've told you underline again and again not to do that! (time)

2 We reached shelter with only seconds to spare before the hurricane arrived. (nick)

3 Orwell needed to use up some spare hours before his interview, so he went to see a movie. (kill)

4 I have hardly any time at the moment. Can I call you back later? (pressed)

5 Jodie had to stop her holiday earlier than planned because of her father's sudden death. (cut)

6 We lost four days' filming because of the weather so we need to work quickly to catch up. (make)

7 Only very rarely do we find a young author with so much talent. (blue)

8 The government ministers are really delaying over reforms to the tax system. (drag)

9 Why don't you stay in my apartment now, perhaps not for long, until you find something else. (time)

10 Lena didn't hurry, but waited patiently until she could find a way to escape. (bide)

WRITING an informal article

6A Underline the less formal alternative of the words/phrases in bold.

CUTTING
IT SHORT

Have you ever wondered why some people are always late? ¹**It is a question/That's something** I often ask myself. ²**I'm always/I am constantly** late for trains, for concerts, for weddings, for everything! I do try, honestly, ³**nevertheless/but** I've been like this all my life.

People hate latecomers. If you arrive late at a meeting ⁴**it is thought/people think** you're lazy or disorganised or you don't actually ⁵**think much of/respect** the other people there. But that isn't true. We time-challenged people live a life of constant anxiety and stress. I can't begin to count the money ⁶**that has been wasted/I've wasted** by missing planes, classes, hair appointments, not to mention the stress of continually apologising for messing up other people's schedules.

However, help is at hand. If you are someone who always cuts things short, here are some suggestions to help you ⁷**get over/recover from** this chronic problem. First of all . . .

B Do you identify with the writer of the article?

C Complete the article with three suggestions and a conclusion (150–200 words).

VOCABULARY manner

1A Add vowels to make words.

1 d__pl__m__t__c
2 c__nfr__nt__t__ __n__l
3 s__ns__bl__
4 s__pp__rt__v__
5 c__ll__b__r__t__v__
6 s__ns__t__v__
7 __nh__lpf__l
8 __ss__rt__v__
9 f__c__ss__d
10 t__ctf__l
11 __ggr__ss__v__
12 d__r__ct

B Which adjectives above are positive (+), negative (-) or can be either (+/-)?

C Match the adjectives in Exercise 1A with quotes 1–10. Sometimes two adjectives are possible.

1 You're late again, Jones! Get into my office and sit down! Now! _____

2 Oh, you look really tired. Lie down and rest, I'll bring you a cup of tea. _____

3 I prefer you in the other dress. This one makes you look overweight. _____

4 You touched the ball! You cheat! _____

5 I'll work on the charts for the report while you edit the text. _____

6 Look, I'm not angry but just tell me, why did Louise get a pay rise but I didn't? _____

7 OK, everyone. I think we're straying from the point. We need to get back to the main issue. _____

8 We don't deal with problems with your connection. You need to phone your broadband provider. You've already tried them? Well, it's nothing to do with us. _____

9 It's true that I don't have the receipt but I only bought it here last week. Could I speak to your supervisor. She's at lunch? No problem, I'll wait. _____

10 If you want to lose weight, don't go on an extreme diet. Just eat slightly less and try and walk for half an hour a day. _____

FUNCTION handling an awkward situation

2A Put the words in the correct order to complete B's part of the conversation.

A: Is everything OK?

B: [1]I've / to / talk / something / about / been / there's / to / you / Actually, / meaning.

_____

A: Oh, is there a problem?

B: [2]you / get / the / to / want / wrong / I / don't / idea, / but …

_____

A: That sounds bad.

B: [3]you / just / mobile / leave / on / that / often / It's / your.

_____

A: I don't understand.

B: [4]you're / annoying / And / it / and / that's / not / rings / when / here.

_____

A: But I need to keep it on in case my son phones.

B: [5]disturbing / trying / but / Yes, / people / are / work / when / to / it's.

_____

A: It's important that he can get straight through to me.

B: [6]I'm / understand / from / see / but / you / where / I / do / coming?

_____

A: I suppose so.

B: [7]set / it / silent / you / when / could / not / to / here / Maybe / you're.

_____

A: What you mean just the 'vibrate' setting?

B: [8]feel / about / you / Yes, / how / would / that?

_____

A: OK, that sounds reasonable. I'll do that from now on. Sorry about that.

B: Thanks, I'd appreciate it.

B ▶ 8.4 Listen to the conversation and repeat B's part. Pay attention to the stress and intonation.

LEARN TO soften a message

3 ▶ 8.5 Listen to B's part of the conversation and add the extra words you hear to the conversation in Exercise 2A.

GRAMMAR conditionals

1 Complete the phrases. Sometimes there is more than one possibility.

A: Looking back over your career so far, [1]you / do / things / differently if you could start again?

B: I'm very happy with my choices so even if I could, [2]I / not / want / change / anything professionally. As far as my personal life is concerned, I do wish I'd waited before settling down. [3]If / Angela and I not / get married so young, then [4]we / still / be / together.

A: And [5]if / you / were / give / advice to me as an up-and-coming actor, [6]what / you / say?

B: [7]If / I / start / again now [8]I / still / think / I / choose to work in the theatre to get as much basic experience as possible.

1 _____	5 _____
2 _____	6 _____
3 _____	7 _____
4 _____	8 _____

GRAMMAR quantifiers

2A Read the descriptions and correct a quantifier in each sentence by crossing out, changing or adding one word.

1 Floor-to-ceiling windows allow you to enjoy lots of fantastic views of the city whilst the city enjoys plenty fantastic views of you.

2 The flat is in need of a little redecoration and lighting but it benefits from a large amount of walls, floors and ceilings.

3 A few flats with such excellent views ever come on the market, and as it is currently owned by an artist, each room is uniquely decorated.

4 The flat would be suitable for either a mushroom grower or someone who loves caves, as the most of the rooms are on the lower ground floor.

5 The flat is in a lively area, close to quite a few shops and several of clubs, so it would benefit from some double glazing in the windows.

B Read the descriptions again. What is the problem with each flat?

VOCABULARY review

3 Complete the sentences with the correct word/phrase.

1 series/serial
a) I can't wait for the next episode of the _____ to find out what happens next.
b) They're doing a _____ on eastern cuisine; last week's was about Thai cooking and next week's is from Malaysia.

2 sitcom/sketch show
a) Al Shaw stars in this _____ about a high-flying executive who suddenly finds himself out of work.
b) Dean Murray is back in the _____ playing his familiar roles as the farmer who can't stand animals, the one-armed dentist and the policeman who can only speak in rhyme.

3 sharpest/lowest ebb
a) He was at his _____ in the winter and only recovered his usual good mood in the spring.
b) She was at her _____ only after she'd had the first coffee of the day.

4 breezy/groggy
a) The medicine made her _____ and irritable.
b) You're looking very bright and _____ . Has something good happened?

5 weighed up/came to
a) They _____ the options and decided to sell the hotel.
b) They examined the situation carefully before they _____ a decision.

6 sticking to/analysing
a) He's _____ his principles and refusing to reveal the name of his informer.
b) He's _____ the situation at the moment.

7 sensitive/sensible
a) She's very _____ to other people's needs.
b) It's _____ to keep a note of your passport number.

8 assertive/tactful
a) You need to be _____ when dealing with him so as not to upset him.
b) You should be more _____ . Don't let her bully you.

4A Look at the underlined sounds in each group. Circle the word with the different sound.

1 b<u>i</u>ased, den<u>y</u>, prom<u>i</u>se

2 r<u>ea</u>lity, thr<u>ea</u>ten, dr<u>ea</u>d

3 <u>s</u>erial, <u>c</u>irculation, <u>a</u>lert

4 per<u>su</u>ade, <u>t</u>abloid, sen<u>s</u>ationalist

5 f<u>o</u>cussed, c<u>o</u>nfrontational, c<u>o</u>lourful

6 sen<u>s</u>ible, aggre<u>ss</u>ive, de<u>s</u>pise

B ▶ RC4.1 **Listen and check. Then listen and repeat.**

FUNCTION handling an awkward situation

5 Underline the correct alternative. In one case both are possible.

A: Ingrid, there's something I've ¹*meant/been meaning* to talk to you about.

B: Sure, Cristina. What's up?

A: I ²*don't want you/hope you don't* take this ³*a wrong/the wrong* way but you often look very tired.

B: What do you mean?

A: ⁴*It's just that/It's that just* I've noticed you yawning sometimes and, well, a receptionist needs to look more welcoming to clients. ⁵*Do you know/Do you see* what I mean?

B: You're right. I have been having difficulties sleeping recently.

A: How ⁶*would you feel/are you feeling* about getting some advice? From your doctor?

B: Yes, that's probably a good idea. Sorry about this, Cristina.

VOCABULARY *PLUS* idioms

6 Cross out two extra words in each sentence.

1 I'm sorry but I'll have to cut it up short as I'm very pressed for my time.

2 For the present time being I'm not saying anything. I'm just biding on my time.

3 The movie companies tend to drag their two feet till the last moment and then suddenly come up with the money in the a nick of time.

4 Time and after time I catch nothing and then once in a the blue moon I land a really big fish.

5 I had to kill my time because Jan was late, and we had to drive really fast to make it up for lost time.

GRAMMAR reported speech

7 Complete the second sentence so that it has a similar meaning to the first. Use between two and five words including the word given.

1 'I want to leave school,' Emilio said to his father.
   TOLD
   Emilio _____ to leave school.

2 'Could you sing something for us?' the guys in the band asked me.
   WANTED
   The guys in the band _____ something for them.

3 You didn't give me your phone number,' Ben said.
   HIM
   Ben explained that I _____ phone number.

4 'Why don't you like computer games?' Jane asked Rick.
   HE
   Jane asked Rick _____ computer games.

5 'Were you working for Sarah at that time?' Harry asked.
   WORKING
   Harry asked me _____ for Sarah at that time.

6 'I won't be seeing Katya until tomorrow,' she said.
   KATYA
   She said she _____ until the next day.

VOCABULARY reporting verbs

8A Match the reporting verbs to the sentences.

agree	admit	apologise	promise	offer
suggest	deny	threaten	~~insist~~	accuse

1   No, I'm paying for the meal. I won't let you. *insist*
2   I'm sorry if I have caused any embarrassment.
3   We'll reduce taxes if you vote for us.
4   Unless I get more money, I'm going to quit the show.
5   You did it Leona! You stole my wallet!
6   We'll share the information with you.
7   Let's take a break for a few minutes.
8   OK, I stole Đ5,000 from the bank.
9   I've never had cosmetic surgery.
10 You want me to make a speech? OK, no problem.

B Complete each sentence above in reported speech using the reporting verbs.

1   He *insisted on paying for the meal*.
2   I _____.
3   We _____.
4   She _____.
5   He _____.
6   They _____.
7   She _____.
8   He _____.
9   He _____.
10 She _____.

GRAMMAR -ing form and infinitive

9 Complete the articles with the correct forms of the verbs.

Right or left: 1

Researchers in the UK have discovered that dogs tend
[1]_____ at the right side of human faces. The right side
is known [2]_____ better at [3]_____ emotional
states. Interestingly, dogs don't seem [4]_____ _____ this
when they look at other animals. [5]_____ human
emotions is an important skill for a pet.

express
do
look
recognise
be

Right or left: 2

In an experiment, 74% of cinema goers would rather
[6]_____ to the right of the screen. The right side of
the brain is important for [7]_____ emotional
information. By [8]_____ the film from the right,
people are choosing [9]_____ themselves the best
viewing experience. Interestingly, when told the film was
poor, people didn't mind [10]_____ a seat anywhere.

have
watch
process
give
sit

VOCABULARY PLUS multi-word verbs

10 Complete the sentences by adding *across*, *back*, *down*, *into*, *out*, *of*, or *up* in the correct place.

1   I'll have to take everything I said about the film.
    It's brilliant!

2   Talks between the two sides have completely
    broken.

3   I don't like her in person but she comes well
    on TV.

4   They're bringing the new version of the game
    next March.

5   He's pulling out the race because of an ankle
    problem.

6   Some old friends in San Francisco put me for
    the night.

7   We want to break the highly competitive youth
    market.

8   The concert turned to be disappointing.

FUNCTION adding emphasis

11 Complete the email extract with different words to complete the phrases that add emphasis.

From: Jo B	To: Emma
Subject: Not happy!	
Date: 7th August	

The people in the flat below us are driving
us [1]_____ crazy. Last Friday they had
an all-night party. I wouldn't have minded
but the thing [2]_____ that they didn't
warn us in advance and there was no
[3]_____ we could sleep through it.
Why [4]_____ earth do people need to
have music so loud? I [5]_____ hate it
when people are [6]_____ thoughtless.
I had [7]_____ a sleepless night that
I was in a bad mood all day and had a
[8]_____ awful argument with Jack. It
ended up with him shouting, 'Well you're
the [9]_____ who wanted to move here
in the first place!' and walking out. Then
the woman downstairs complained to
me about the shouting! That made me
[10]_____ furious!

TEST

Circle the correct option to complete the sentences.

1 That's not very _____ – telling her she's put on weight!

a) collaborative   b) unhelpful   c) tactful

2 There were _____ things I would have changed but not many.

a) quite a few   b) a few   c) very few

3 The doctor told _____ to bed.

a) that I should go   b) me to go   c) me going

4 They _____ doing it.

a) insisted on   b) threatened   c) apologised

5 Pilots need to be _____ so the maximum flying time is 100 hours a month.

a) wide   b) alert   c) a spring in their step

6 My grandfather asked me _____ recently.

a) what had I been doing   b) what I'd been doing
c) if I'd been doing

7 It's not easy to see, but _____ some kind of animal.

a) I'd say it's   b) might be   c) it looks as

8 It was _____ fantastic news that I couldn't believe it at first.

a) such   b) so   c) such a

9 You need to _____ the pros and cons.

a) follow   b) go against   c) weigh up

10 If Tom hadn't acted so quickly they _____ now.

a) might have been killed   b) weren't alive
c) could be dead

11 _____ to go to the gym twice a week.

a) I persuaded   b) It's not worth   c) My aim is

12 _____ do it slowly or you could cut yourself.

a) You should learn   b) You'd better   c) Practise

13 I like factual programmes so I don't watch _____ .

a) documentaries   b) current affairs programmes
c) reality shows

14 There is _____ traffic on the road because of the weather.

a) hardly   b) very little   c) a small number of

15 Thousands of people _____ to vote.

a) turned out   b) brought out   c) pulled out

16 Margit said _____ the next day.

a) she'll do it   b) she'd do it   c) she's doing it

17 You often _____ good websites while you're looking for something else.

a) put up with   b) come across   c) break into

18 I _____ him to phone Washington.

a) suggested   b) offered   c) reminded

19 Would Kurt _____ finding a new job?

a) consider   b) need   c) expect

20 Louise Becker's _____ is read by millions of people every day.

a) columnist   b) editorial   c) readership

21 You're _____ wanted to come!

a) one who   b) the one who   c) the one

22 I don't want _____ get the wrong idea, but …

a) that you   b) you to   c) you

23 The paper has been accused of being _____ .

a) biased   b) tabloid   c) sensationalism

24 How long do you think it will take for them to _____ a decision?

a) come to   b) arrive   c) stick to

25 If you _____ the lottery ticket, we'd be rich now.

a) don't lose   b) didn't lose   c) hadn't lost

26 I _____ whenever I see that photo!

a) cringe   b) despise with a passion   c) 'm fussed

27 If you'd been in my situation, what _____ ?

a) would you do   b) would you have done
c) did you do

28 Hurry up. We've got to _____ time.

a) kill some   b) make up for lost
c) be pressed for

29 _____ ticket costs Ð20.

a) Each   b) Few   c) All

30 It's OK to speak your mind but why are you always so _____ ?

a) focussed   b) assertive   c) confrontational

TEST RESULT **/30**

LISTENING

1A Look at the pictures. Can you think of a reason why you might NOT notice the animals?

B ▶ 9.1 Listen to the first part of a radio programme and answer the questions.

1 What is the best definition of 'inattentional blindness'?
   a) Losing your eyesight because of someone's carelessness
   b) Failing to see things that are obvious because you are stressed
   c) Not seeing one thing because you are focussed on something else
2 Were your ideas about the pictures right?

C ▶ 9.2 Listen to the rest of the programme and put the topics in the correct order. One topic is mentioned twice and one is not mentioned.

a) pilots
b) motorcyclists
c) drivers
d) footballers
e) store security guards

D Listen again to the whole programme. Are the statements true (T), false (F) or is the information not given (NG)?

1 A quarter of the people who did the gorilla experiment didn't notice the gorilla.
2 If you're looking for someone with glasses, you might not notice someone with a parrot.
3 Drivers who are sending text messages might not notice a car stopping in front of them.
4 If you expect to see a particular word or name on a sign, you might not notice a synonym.
5 In a simulation, trained pilots were better at seeing unusual things on the runway than non-pilots.
6 A thief is more likely to fool a guard in a store by stealing openly.
7 It's safer to drive a car than to ride a motorcycle.
8 The expert gives the advice 'Expect the unexpected'.

GRAMMAR -ing form and infinitive

2A Underline the correct alternative.

1a) After high school, I went on *finding/to find* work in order to earn money.
  b) After high school, I went on *studying/to study* and attended university because that was expected.

2a) I remember *locking/to lock* my flat when I left it today, but it's possible that I didn't do it.
  b) I remembered *locking/to lock* my flat when I left it today, I'm 100 percent sure.

3a) I'm trying *learning/to learn* English well enough to pass an advanced exam.
  b) I tried *speaking/to speak* English in case they understood it but they didn't.

4a) I'll never forget *meeting/to meet* my English teacher for the first time.
  b) I've forgotten *doing/to do* my homework many times.

5a) I had to stop *thinking/to think* about all of these sentences before answering.
  b) I've had to stop *thinking/to think* about my other work so that I could concentrate on this exercise.

6a) I like *studying/to study* English at least fifteen minutes a day even if I'm not in the mood.
  b) I like *travelling/to travel* more than anything else.

B Tick the sentences above that are true for you.

3 Complete the story with the correct form of the verbs in brackets.

MY DAY AS A POLICE WITNESS

It was 2009 and I had witnessed a theft – in fact, I'd tried ¹_____ (catch) the thief, but when I caught up with him he pulled out a knife, so I stopped ²_____ (chase) him and walked away. I remember ³_____ (stand) there, thinking how silly the situation was, before I gave up. I like ⁴_____ (be) helpful even when it's unpleasant or dangerous, so I didn't mind. Before I walked away though, I remembered ⁵_____ (memorise) his face, in case the police asked me for a description; but I made a mistake, because I forgot ⁶_____ (pay) attention to his height. Well, the police did call me a few days later and said they'd caught the guy and needed me to identify him in a line-up. So I went in, and looked at the eight faces … they asked me which was the thief, but I just went on ⁷_____ (look) at the faces, because they ALL looked like the thief. I tried ⁸_____ (picture) him with my eyes closed, but it didn't work. In the end I picked someone – the biggest, tallest one – because that was my recollection, that the guy was big and threatening. The one I picked turned out to be a police officer himself (who later went on ⁹_____ (become) the chief of police), and the real thief was the shortest guy in the line-up. On my way out, I stopped ¹⁰_____ (say) goodbye to the head detective, and he just said 'Don't call us, we'll call you.'

VOCABULARY crime

4A Find twelve words for crimes in the wordsearch.

P	I	C	K	P	O	C	K	E	T	I	N	G
S	H	O	P	L	I	F	T	I	N	G	I	W
U	A	U	U	R	U	Z	T	K	X	K	D	J
V	A	N	D	A	L	I	S	M	W	D	E	R
T	B	T	A	X	E	V	A	S	I	O	N	Q
M	R	E	E	I	T	Z	T	R	S	X	T	N
U	I	R	I	D	N	N	F	R	R	I	N	
G	B	F	P	T	X	T	T	I	Z	Z	T	T
G	E	E	H	A	C	K	I	N	G	H	Y	A
I	R	I	S	T	A	L	K	I	N	G	T	R
N	Y	T	I	P	K	C	T	Y	B	U	H	S
G	K	I	D	N	A	P	P	I	N	G	E	O
N	V	N	H	Q	G	X	S	X	W	Y	F	N
I	M	G	A	L	C	U	C	P	V	H	T	Z

B Complete the sentences with the criminal connected to ten crimes above.

1 That fire wasn't an accident, it was started by a well-known _____.

2 She was being followed by a _____ and had to get bodyguards to protect her.

3 A _____ somehow got into my computer and stole my bank information.

4 The _____ are demanding a ransom of £1 million for the boy.

5 Some _____ have sprayed graffiti on the wall of the school and broken a number of windows.

6 I hated working in the department store as we lost more things to _____ than we sold to customers.

7 I was walking home late when a _____ pulled out a knife and took all my things.

8 Robson wasn't just a graphic designer, he was also a _____ who made fake money as a sideline.

9 Oh no! A _____'s taken my wallet. I was on a bus and I never felt a thing!

10 A new TV campaign is encouraging people to inform the tax authorities about _____. Apparently billions of euros are owed by people who haven't paid their taxes.

C ▶ 9.3 Listen and write the words according to their stress pattern. Then listen and repeat.

Oo   *arson*

Ooo

Oooo

oOooo

FIVE REASONS YOU'LL FALL FOR AN INTERNET SCAM

a) pride
b) greed c) sympathy
d) fear e) curiosity

Most of us think we're too clever to be caught by an email scam, but hustlers know they can always find someone naive enough to fall for their tricks. They also know five key facts about human nature, and one of these is behind every email scam you'll come across:

1 _____: You would think people would learn, but the desire for more money is our greatest *vulnerability*. From the instant lottery ('You've already won!') to an inheritance from the relative you never knew you had, the scam always aims at the same thing: to get you to pay in advance in the hope that you'll get back ten or a hundred times that much later

2 _____: It's amazing how many of us imagine we've written a great novel, or at least a good poem, and have such a strong desire for *recognition* that we'd actually pay for it. The publishing scam works in clever stages, starting with a simple request to submit your poem. You then find out it's been chosen as a semi-finalist in a poetry contest; you only need to send in some money to register. Eventually you're asked for a large amount of cash to cover travel costs so that you can go and receive your prize at the (non-existent) presentation ceremony!

3 _____: If you find yourself paying for a 'premium subscription' to a service that promises to give you access to information – about yourself or someone else – you might be paying for a genuine, functioning service, but it might just be another scam that *preys on* your desire to know more. These often start out by telling you that THEY have information about YOU, and that you can protect that information by subscribing; or they offer information about anyone you want. There *are* agencies that really do sell personal information (for example credit ratings), but many of these offers are *bogus*.

4 _____: The email may contain a direct threat with an equally direct demand for money, or it may be more *subtle* and tell you that your bank account has been attacked and you must enter your personal details, including your PIN, to protect it; or that your email account will be cancelled unless you verify your password. Of course once the scammers have this information, they can get to your money, or pretend they're you and use that disguise to get money.

5 _____: Who can ignore a photograph of a suffering child, or the *plight* of disaster victims in need? Sadly, for every *legitimate* charity in operation there are probably dozens of fake charities using our natural kindness and compassion to get us to transfer money to a bank account somewhere, but the end result is that we're just making millionaires out of the scammers.

So, if you've received an email from an *unverifiable* source and you're feeling greed, pride, curiosity, fear or sympathy, you're probably being scammed.

READING

1A Complete the article with the five emotion words a)–e).

B The quotes are from people who fell for one of the scams in the article. Write the correct number of each scam next to the sentences.

a) That's strange, I can't access my email anymore.

b) I sent the subscription form in and the money last week. They haven't replied yet.

c) Everyone should give something, we can't just let them starve.

d) Look at this. I've got an uncle in Italy. Or I used to have one.

e) Excuse me, I'm here for the awards. I believe there's a room booked in my name.

C Match the meanings 1–8 with the word/phrase in italics in the article.

1 takes advantage of

2 it really exists and it's legal

3 unfortunate situation

4 fame

5 clever and indirect

6 you can't check it

7 weakness

8 fake

VOCABULARY synonyms

2A Read the forum entries. Which thing do you think is the worst?

WHAT'S THE WORST THING YOU DID WHEN YOU WERE A KID?

- We went door to door and we would ¹**pose as** boy scouts raising money for a charity. We used to ²**fool** everyone, but it wasn't hard – we had the right uniforms.

- I used to ³**swap** my neighbour's newspaper every day for the previous day's paper. He never noticed.

- My friend and I took sweets from the local shop. One of us would ⁴**divert** the shopkeeper's attention while the other filled her bag ...

- I used to ask people for change and when they took it out of their pocket I'd ⁵**snatch** it and run away.

- I told people I'd been robbed and needed two euros to get home. They used to ⁶**fall for it** every time, and I made at least ten euros an hour.

B Put the letters in order to make synonyms. The first letter is underlined.

a) sa<u>d</u>ttric	_____	d) <u>b</u>rag	_____
b) ce<u>d</u>ivee	_____	e) cwith<u>s</u>	_____
c) <u>n</u>edterp ot eb	_____	f) <u>e</u>b keant ni	_____

C Match words/phrases in bold in Exercise 2A with synonyms a)–f) above.

GRAMMAR past modals of deduction

3 Underline the correct alternative. Sometimes there is more than one possibility.

A: You ¹*might have/must have/should have* left the car unlocked. The doors are open, no windows are broken, and my bag's gone!

B: I thought I'd locked it but I ²*might have/can't have/shouldn't have* left it open. I clearly remember locking it.

A: Or the thief ³*could have/must have/should have* been good at picking locks.

4 Complete the sentences with a past modal of deduction and a suitable verb.

1 They _____ home yet – they only left half an hour ago and it's 60 km away.

2 Ali and Fatima _____ each other in college; they're always talking about their time there.

3 You _____ your keys when you took out your wallet or maybe you left them in the café.

4 This essay is too good to be Leila's own work; it _____ from the internet.

5 I _____ my hand when I was peeling the potatoes or maybe later.

6 But you _____ him in town yesterday – he's been abroad for a week.

VOCABULARY PLUS
dependent prepositions

5A Complete the news stories by adding the dependent prepositions *for, from, of* and *with* to the verbs in bold. The prepositions don't always follow the verbs immediately.

> **February 5th** – An Edinburgh man was **charged** murder today. Police say they **suspect** 48-year-old Bill Haller committing a series of murders but a senior police officer says they will only **accuse** Haller one, the famous Scarsdale murder.

> **February 9th** – A police car transporting prisoner Bill Haller crashed on the motorway today and burst into flames. Haller managed to **rescue** the driver the burning vehicle just before it exploded. The mayor **thanked** the prisoner **saving** the driver (who by coincidence is the mayor's son) from certain death.

> **February 11th** – Bill Haller was **cleared** the Scarsdale murder today as police **arrested** another suspect the murder. The mayor **praised** the police their detective work and **apologised** to Haller the mistake. Haller made a statement **criticising** the police their actions and **blamed** an ambitious senior police officer charging him without evidence.

B Read the stories again. Why do you think the man was released?

WRITING a leaflet; avoiding repetition

6A Put the words in order to complete the tips for how to keep secure at an ATM.

1 nearby / you / make / characters / sure / check / suspicious / that / there / no / are

   Make sure you check that there are no suspicious characters nearby.

2 your / your / entering / be / cover / fingers / careful / PIN / when / particularly / to

   _____

3 count / to / try / quickly / money / the

   _____

4 your / put / to / time / take / safely / away / card

   _____

5 if / to / attention / around / tries / your / turn / someone / get / never

   _____

6 be / nearby / always / people / of / aware

   _____

B Write six tips for a leaflet: *How to avoid being a victim of pickpocketers.* Use a variety of ways to give the advice.

FUNCTION reporting an incident

1A Find the mistakes in the underlined phrases and write the correct versions below.

A: I've just been robbed, on the underground. By a pickpocket.

B: What happened?

A: Well, this guy got on the train and ¹he reminded me to that English football player … ²wait, my mind's gone blink. Oh yeah, David Beckham.

B: David Beckham? Didn't you wonder why he was travelling on the underground?

A: ³It never occupied me, no. Well, then everyone crowded round with their phonecams.

B: Typical!

A: I had to push my way past them and ⁴before I was realising what was happening my wallet was gone, right out of my bag.

B: Did you see or feel anyone take it?

A: ⁵No, in fact only it was a minute later that I realised they'd done it. ⁶It was all happened so fast, and I was in a hurry anyway.

B: So the David Beckham lookalike must have been a distraction?

A: Yeah, and he must have had someone working with him.

B: Well, the people with phonecams, maybe they …

A: Do you think so? ⁷They seemed to like students, but …

B: Oh, definitely, it was a pickpocket gang. That's how they work.

1 _____

2 _____

3 _____

4 _____

5 _____

6 _____

7 _____

B ▶ 9.4 **Listen and check. Then listen and say A's part at the same time as the recording.**

VOCABULARY incidents

2 Complete the account of a bad dream with one word in each gap.

I was cooking when I heard a loud crash outside. I went out to see what it was – a driver had tried to avoid knocking ¹_____ a penguin crossing the road and had run ²_____ a second penguin who was just behind the first one. I was trying to help when the driver pointed at my window and I saw that the frying pan was on ³_____ . I tried the door but I realised I'd locked myself ⁴_____ so I picked up the first penguin and tried to use it to break ⁵_____ the door. Its wings suddenly grew huge and it flew off so then I tried to climb in through the bathroom window but I got ⁶_____ . The driver pulled me out and for some reason I then decided to climb onto the roof but I lost my balance and fell ⁷_____ . I must have got knocked ⁸_____ because the next thing I remember was opening my eyes and seeing Brad Pitt standing there with an empty bottle saying, 'Sorry, we've run out of water'. Then I woke up!

LEARN TO rephrase

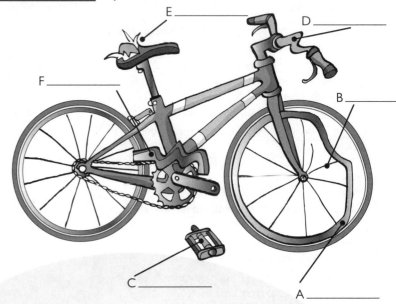

3A Label the parts of the bicycle A–F with the words in the box.

| pedal | chain guard | handlebar | spokes | rim | saddle |

B ▶ 9.5 **Listen to the conversation or read the audio script on page 81 to check.**

READING

1A Look at the photo and read the question on the forum. How would you answer it? Can you give an example?

B Read the forum and match comments 1–7 with categories a)–d).

a) sound /
b) image
c) situation
d) other

C Seven sentences have been removed from the article. Choose from sentences 1–7 the one which fits each gap a)–g).

1 I guess I identify with the character from the start, and so it feels like it's me who's trapped.

2 Maybe it reminds me of my early childhood, that feeling of being lost, of hearing my own voice crying out for help.

3 And then there's that fast bit in *Friday the 13th*, they have the whole orchestra playing ...

4 Darkness and shadow can have the same effect – the effect of hiding the evil character but letting you see just enough to imagine its shape and form.

5 You know that partly because they're not a main character and they're not needed to play the story out.

6 It's similar I guess when there's a sinister little boy or girl ... or twins in old-fashioned clothes ...

7 Some are also made from made-up compound nouns, like *Cloverfield*, *Skinwalkers*, *Wickerhouse*.

D Find a word in the forum that means:

1 make a high-pitched sound (paragraph 1)

_____

2 strange and frightening (paragraph 3)

_____

3 damaged or made immoral (paragraph 4)

_____

4 talking quickly (paragraph 6)

_____

5 quick moment (paragraph 7)

_____

FILM FAN FORUM

This week we asked:

What makes a horror film scary for you?

1 I'm a big fan of horror film music, and I think that's the thing that really carries the fear factor for me. You get slow creepy music like in *Jaws*, you know buh-dup-buh-dup-buh-dup-buh-dup … (a)___ or the screaming shock music like in *Psycho*, where suddenly when the shower curtain opens, the violins shriek incredibly loudly. Every time I see that scene I jump out of my seat, and it's the music that does it.

2 Vulnerability is what gets me. A character is put into a position where they can't really protect themselves against something terrible, whether they're alone, trapped in a closed space, or walking down a dark stairway or narrow hallway, or in a forest that's overgrown and hard to walk through, and basically not knowing what's going on, but knowing it's not good. (b)___

3 I think the title of a film has quite an impact. If it's good, it somehow captures the whole experience of the film, so even years after seeing *The Omen*, if I heard that title, I'd relive the feeling. The really good titles seem to follow a pattern, for example 'the' followed by a word ending with *-ing*, for example *The Haunting*, *The Shining*, *The Vanishing*. (c)___ Or you get odd, eerie words after 'the': *The Ring*, *The Uninvited*, and of course *The Omen*. Very scary, I don't know why.

4 A kid's bicycle upside-down with one of its wheels turning. A broken doll. A child's shoe. I see a shot of one of those and I hide under my seat. (d)___ I think it has to do with the innocence of childhood being corrupted by evil.

5 There's a kind of scene in a lot of horror films that always gets me. I call it the 'innocent victim' scene. You'll have a character who's often a very likeable old guy or old lady who does a simple job like running a shop or working in a restaurant. What happens is something like they close up the shop, get into their car, drive home in darkness, pull into their driveway ... and so on, and you know that at any moment something very bad is going to happen to them, but you don't know exactly when. (e)___

6 When the sound track has sound effects that sound a bit like human voices, that really scares me. So like religious chants, or women's voices chattering. You almost hear words but not quite. Oh, a child's voice, that gives me the shivers. (f)___

7 When you get just a glimpse of the villain or evil being. So he or she walks by a window, or is spotted by a character just for a flash, and then is out of sight. (g)___ It really makes the evil come alive in your mind, because your imagination starts racing, generating images.

VOCABULARY adjectives to describe films

2A Add vowels to make words.

1 f__st-p__c__d	6 p__ __gn__nt	11 gr__pp__ng
2 ch__ll__ng	7 __l__ctr__fy__ng	12 w__ __k
3 d__ll	8 br__ll__ __nt	13 t__ __ch__ng
4 m__v__ng	9 h__rr__f__c	14 cr__ __py
5 __w__s__m__	10 pr__d__ct__bl__	15 __nf__rg__tt__bl__

B Draw lines to connect the five sets of similar adjectives. There are three words in each set.

GRAMMAR relative clauses

3A Underline the correct alternative. Sometimes there is more than one possibility.

✋ my - blog ✋

my - home ☞

my - life ☞

my - photos ☞

THE PROBLEM WITH CINEMAS

Until recently, one thing ¹*what/that/which* I used to do was to go and see new films as soon as they came out. But I've stopped because of the way ²*who/what/that* people behave there. The cinema should be a place ³*which/where/that* you can be transported to another world, but this is impossible because:

- a mobile phone rings, ⁴*when/which/that* completely kills the moment. People ⁵*who/that/what* leave their mobile phones on are careless; people ⁶*who/whose/when* phones ring should be sent out.

- people act like they're at home, by ⁷*whom/where/which* I mean they have conversations, sometimes ⁸*where/when/that* there's something really moving happening on screen. You hear about everything ⁹*what/that/which* they've been doing for the last day instead of the dialogue.

- children, ¹⁰*that/who's/whose* parents should control them better, kick your seat every time they laugh.

B In which examples above is it possible to leave out the relative pronoun?

_____

4 Make sentences containing relative clauses with the prompts. The word in bold immediately follows the relative pronoun.

1 A biopic / be / a film / **tells** / the life story / famous person.
A biopic is a film which tells the life story of a famous person.

2 The biopic / I want to review today / be / *Raging Bull,* / **be** / the story of a famous boxer.

_____

3 Robert de Niro, / **play** / the part of Jake La Motta, / be / absolutely extraordinary.

_____

4 The film / be / made at a time / **most** biopics / be of heroic figures.

_____

5 The film, / **be** / directed by Martin Scorsese, / be / now recognised as a masterpiece.

_____

6 De Niro / become / interested when he read the book / on / **story** / be / based.

_____

LEARN TO write descriptively

5A Rearrange the letters to make adverbs that collocate with the past participles.

1 ghlhyi _____ / ylediw _____ praised

2 hyhlars _____ / oyghlwelrminve _____ / eahvliy _____ criticised

3 klulfysil _____ / iisetvsynle _____ directed

4 ptlnnoagyi _____ / nlngvnoiicyc _____ acted

B Complete the sentences with one of the collocations above.

1a) Audiences all over the world have applauded the film.
The film has been _____.

b) Critics have given it very positive reviews.
It has been _____.

2a) There wasn't a critic who said a positive thing about his last movie.
His last movie was _____.

b) The reviews weren't just negative, they were <u>very</u> negative.
The film was _____.

3a) It wasn't an easy script, but Spielberg showed his talent in the way he directed it.
The script was _____.

b) The topic is a delicate one, but Bigelow showed she could handle this in her direction of the film.
The film was _____.

4a) The acting in that scene made me cry.
That scene was _____.

b) Morgan Freeman's acting was so good, I actually believed he was the real Nelson Mandela.
The role of Nelson Mandela was _____.

GRAMMAR participle clauses

1A Read the article and circle one mistake in each picture.

DAMAGED GOODS

When a woman ¹*took/taking* an art class at a New York museum tripped and fell into a Picasso painting, ²*tear/tearing* a fifteen-centimetre hole in the canvas, the public gasped and giggled, ³*shocked/shocking* at how anyone could get so close to a valuable work of art. But museums, ⁴*pressed/pressing* to attract as many paying customers as possible, often give visitors considerable access to works of art and this can carry risks. Similar incidents have happened in other collections:

- A visitor ⁵*walked/walking* down the stairs in a Cambridge museum stumbled into some 17th century Chinese vases, ⁶*shattered/shattering* the vases into hundreds of pieces.
- A drawing by a famous artist, ⁷*valued/valuing* at over £80,000, was put through a paper shredder by a worker at a London auction house. The worker, deeply ⁸*embarrassed/embarrassing* by the incident, has managed to keep his (or her) identity a secret.
- A housekeeper ⁹*employed/employing* by a wealthy German family ¹⁰*lived/living* in a villa near Berlin knocked down a Ming dynasty plate.
- A painting by the Italian, Giorgio de Chirico, ¹¹*displayed/displaying* in a house in the Netherlands, was damaged when a demolition ball came through the wall, ¹²*put/putting* a large hole through the painting.
- At the London National Gallery a painting ¹³*was/being* removed from a wall was broken in two. Apparently the glue ¹⁴*used/using* to hold sections of the frame wasn't strong enough.

B Underline the correct alternatives in the article in Exercise 1A.

2A Replace the underlined phrases with participles. Add commas or make any other changes to the rest of the sentence where necessary.

1 The people <u>who lived</u> on the other side of the river were trapped.
   The people living on the other side of the river were trapped.

2 Anyone <u>who is planning</u> to go home early or <u>who wants</u> to take a break should let us know.
   _____

3 <u>As I walked</u> out of the restaurant, I ran into my old boss, <u>who was coming</u> in.
   _____

4 I used to work with the woman <u>who lives</u> next door.
   _____

5 I left the party quickly <u>and didn't tell</u> anyone that I was unwell.
   _____

6 <u>She carried</u> a child under each arm and ran out of the blazing building.
   _____

7 He jumped up <u>because he was frightened</u> by the loud bang, <u>as he mistook</u> the door for a gun.
   _____

8 Walls <u>which have been painted</u> white tend to attract more graffiti.
   _____

B ▶ 10.1 Listen and check. Then listen and say the sentences at the same time as the recording, paying attention to stress and intonation.

VOCABULARY the arts

3 Add vowels to make words.
1 We couldn't get tickets, the show was a s _ ll- _ _ t.
2 He's what they call an ' _ lt _ rn _ t _ v _ ' comedian, which means I wouldn't take my grandmother to see him!
3 The film has got r _ v _ r _ v _ _ ws in most papers.
4 It was a gr _ _ nd-br _ _ king performance. Completely different from anything I've seen before.
5 The show is amazing! A real m _ st-s _ _ !
6 Her interpretation of the role of Juliet has cr _ _ t _ d _ st _ r amongst the critics.
7 They stopped playing small clubs once they went m _ _ nstr _ _ m and became too popular.
8 The musical was a fl _ p and closed after one week.
9 I don't know what all the hyp _ was about. She was awful!
10 The main dancer was ill and someone else took his place, which was a real l _ td _ wn.

LISTENING

4A Look at the photos. Which one do you think is better and why? Think of three reasons.

B ▶ 10.2 Listen to Part 1 of a talk about how to take a good photo and circle the best alternative.

1 The main problem with the light is that:
   a) it's behind the photographer.
   b) it's shining into the subject's eyes.
   c) it's too direct and creates a flat effect.

2 The fact that the subject's head is in the centre:
   a) is good because it's in sharp focus.
   b) is bad because it leaves space above.
   c) is bad because it cuts off her legs.

3 The problem with the background is that:
   a) it's not interesting.
   b) it's not completely in focus.
   c) it's a missed opportunity.

4 The person taking the picture:
   a) zoomed in too close.
   b) is standing too far away.
   c) didn't look at the woman's face carefully.

5 The last problem is that:
   a) the woman is looking at the camera.
   b) the photographer is too tall.
   c) the camera is looking down at the woman.

C ▶ 10.3 Listen to Part 2 and complete the notes. Use no more than three words for each sentence.

THE FIVE RULES

1 *Position yourself so that the light is coming* _____.

2 *Divide the screen into* _____ *and place the subject at one of the* _____.

3 *Make sure the background is* _____.

4 *The distance to the subject should be* _____.

5 *Adjust your* _____ *so that the lens and the subject's eyes are* _____.

VOCABULARY *PLUS* two-part phrases

5A Complete the advice for studying English.

Do you ever get sick and ¹_____ **of feeling you're not making progress?** Everybody who learns a language has their ups and ²_____ along the way. Follow our dos and ³_____ for language study and we guarantee your English will improve in leaps and ⁴_____!

DO find a place with peace and ⁵_____ to do your studying.

DON'T study off and ⁶_____, skipping days, or you'll make much slower progress. Spend at least ten minutes a day doing something in English, even just studying words.

DO watch a film in English now and ⁷_____, at least once a month, and don't worry about understanding every word – just enjoy it!

DO record yourself in English once in a while and listen to the recording. Most mobile phones can make a rough and ⁸_____ recording that's good enough for this task.

DO speak English with anyone who will speak English with you, even if their English is not as good as yours. There are pros and ⁹_____ to practising with someone below your level, but in fact it can be very valuable because you'll be thinking in English.

DON'T look back and ¹⁰_____ between an exercise and the key when doing a workbook exercise. Do the whole exercise and THEN look at the key.

DO learn from your mistakes. When you do a test or exam, go back and study the exam through and ¹¹_____ and think about how to improve weak areas.

There's lots more advice, we could go on and ¹²_____ but you should really get back to studying!

B Tick which advice you think is good.

FUNCTION giving a tour

1A Put the words in the correct order.

1 visit / worth / It's / a / well

_____

2 the / over / Let's / to / head

_____

3 to / they / interrupt / had / Supposedly,

_____

4 not, / or / it / Believe / took / it

_____

5 was / as / originally / It / built

_____

6 were / Well, / founded / they / in

_____

7 our / retrace / Let's / to / steps

_____

8 he / that / goes / story / The / used

_____

B ▶10.4 Listen and draw any links between the words in the phrases. Then listen and repeat.

It's well wor͡th a͡ visit

C Complete the conversation with phrases from Exercise 1A. Write the number of the phrase in the correct place.

A: Here we are at the famous Leaning Tower of Pisa. (a)___ a bell-tower for the cathedral.

B: It looks like it's going to fall over!

A: It won't. Not today. (b)___ 177 years to build.

B: Why did it take so long?

A: (c)___ its construction because Pisa was constantly at war.

B: Didn't Galileo live in Pisa?

A: Yes. (d)___ the leaning tower to demonstrate the rules of gravity, by dropping things off the top.

B: Is that true?

A: Who knows, really. (e)___ Piazza dei Cavalieri.

B: Oh yes, that's such a beautiful square.

A: Well, my favourite restaurant, Ristorante alle Bandierine, is on the way. (f)___

B: Sounds good to me.

VOCABULARY dimensions

2A Write the noun and verb forms of each adjective.

1 long *length*   *lengthen*

2 short _____ _____

3 narrow _____ _____

4 wide _____ _____

5 thin _____ _____

6 thick _____ _____

7 low _____ _____

8 high _____ _____

9 large _____ _____

B Complete the sentences with the correct form of the words above.

1 The jury needs to _____ down its choices before choosing the finalists.

2 He used to have such a thick head of hair, it's really beginning to _____.

3 People believe the voting age should be _____ from eighteen to sixteen.

4 The _____ of the mixture is important and it shouldn't be too thin, so when you mix together the flour and water, wait for it to _____ before pouring it into the pan.

5 The _____ of the road isn't enough to add another lane – they'll have to _____ it.

6 We need to check the _____ of the sofa to make sure it's not too long.

7 Lessons should be shorter and they should _____ the breaks in between.

8 This video tutorial will show you how to _____ a small photo.

9 The bridge was _____ enough for normal trucks to go underneath, but the _____ of those particular lorries was above the legal limit.

10 This exercise is too long; it needs to be _____.

LEARN TO express estimates

3 Correct the mistakes in the sentences.

1 There were under just 200 people at the party.

2 The homework should take you rough an hour to do.

3 We'll be arriving at 4 o'clock or so what?

4 The renovations cost downwards of one million euros.

5 We're expecting somewhere on a region of a thousand people for the conference.

GRAMMAR -ing form and infinitive

1 Underline the correct alternative.

The rules of dinner party etiquette for women (1950)

Dining in high society can be stressful if you don't know the rules. Study these and you'll survive any dinner party …

1 When you are about to sit down, stop *letting/to let* the man next to you hold the chair for you.

2 Once seated, remember *turning/to turn* to your right and start a conversation with the man next to you.

3 If the man has forgotten *turning/to turn* to his left, gracefully join the conversation on your left and always try *looking/to look* interested even if you are not.

4 If another guest tells you they remember *meeting/to meet* you before and you in fact forget *meeting/to meet* them, just agree with them.

5 If someone drops a dish, don't stop *talking/to talk*, just go on *having/to have* the conversation you were having.

6 If the person you're talking to doesn't seem to be listening, try *asking/to ask* questions – people love talking about themselves!

Next week: Tips for men!

GRAMMAR participle clauses

2 Complete the articles with the present or past participle of an appropriate verb.

Numbers: people

5.5 litres: the amount of blood
[1]_____ in the human body.
13: the percentage of the world's population
[2]_____ in deserts.
25: the number of years [3]_____ asleep if you live to seventy-five.
70: the number of muscles [4]_____ to say a single word.
30,000: the number of people [5]_____ each year by cobras and vipers.

| spend |
| use |
| live |
| find |
| kill |

Numbers: machines

40: the percentage of spam email
[6]_____ at addresses [7]_____ with A, M, S, R or P.
53: the percentage of people [8]_____ from nomophobia (fear of being without their mobiles).
100: the number of cars [9]_____ every minute.
14,528: the number of text messages
[10]_____ by a Californian girl in one month.

| suffer |
| send |
| make |
| start |
| arrive |

VOCABULARY review

3 Complete the sentences with the correct word/ phrase.

1 deceive/fall for

   a) I always _____ his compliments even though I know he just wants a favour.

   b) It's not difficult to _____ people because most of us want to believe that everyone's intentions are good.

2 taken in/distracted

   a) They were _____ by us pretending to have a fight.

   b) Everyone was _____ by the trick, and no one saw the guy robbing the cash register.

3 ground-breaking/sell-out

   a) It was a _____ performance and changed the way people saw the character of Hamlet forever.

   b) It was a _____ performance and impossible to get tickets for.

4 letdown/flop

   a) After the success of their first album, the mild response to their second one was a _____.

   b) They were booked for five shows but the first was a total _____ so the rest were cancelled.

5 bribery/tax evasion

   a) _____ is common in the country, which is why if you have money you can get anything done.

   b) _____ is normal for most people, which is why there is a big hole in the government's finances.

6 stalkers/vandals

   a) Celebrities often have to deal with _____ who follow them and try to make contact.

   b) Some _____ sprayed graffiti on the shop windows and broke the sign over the door.

7 breadth/depth

   a) As the _____ of the river changed, they had to build a longer bridge.

   b) In the past the _____ of a lake was measured with a rope lowered to the bottom.

8 lower/shorten

   a) We'll need to _____ the time it takes to get the produce from the farm to the supermarket.

   b) If you want us to listen to you, you'll have to _____ your salary demands.

9 moving/gripping

   a) I find the plot of all of his books so _____ that I can't put them down once I start reading.

   b) I never expected an animated film to be so _____ – I actually found myself with tears in my eyes.

10 knocked out/knocked over

   a) He got _____ when his head hit the ice; he had to be taken to hospital.

   b) He got _____ during the football match but he picked himself up straightaway and carried on.

4A Look at the underlined sounds in each group. Circle the word with the different sound.

1 resc<u>ue</u>, t<u>ou</u>ching, m<u>u</u>gging

2 h<u>y</u>pe, h<u>ei</u>ght, ch<u>i</u>lling

3 p<u>oi</u>gnant, n<u>ow</u> and then, gr<u>ou</u>nd-breaking

4 rave rev<u>iew</u>s, acc<u>u</u>se, d<u>u</u>ll

5 h<u>a</u>cker, c<u>au</u>se, f<u>a</u>ll for

6 <u>e</u>lectrifying, brib<u>e</u>ry, d<u>e</u>ceive

B ▶ RC5.1 Listen and check. Then listen and repeat.

GRAMMAR past modals of deduction

5A Read the two puzzles. What do you think the answers are? Write two ideas for each.

Puzzle ❶ A fully booked 747 took off from Hong Kong, bound for London Heathrow. When it arrived in London, there were no passengers on board.

Puzzle ❷ There were two men who were born on the same day in the same hospital. They had the same mother and the same last name. They looked exactly alike. But they weren't twins.

B Complete the conversation about the puzzles with *must/might/could/can't/couldn't have*.

A: OK, so what about the plane puzzle?

B: The people [1]_____ (get) on the plane.

A: They did get on.

B: Then I'm not sure, but the plane [2]_____ (experience) a problem and everyone had to get off.

A: No, there was no problem with the plane. I'll give you a hint: it wasn't a non-stop flight.

B: Got it! The plane [3]_____ (make) a stop on the way, and all the passengers got off there.

A: That's right. So what about the second puzzle?

B: That can't be right, the woman [4]_____ (give) birth to twins!

A: No, as it says, they weren't twins.

B: Oh. Then they [5]_____ (have) the same birthday, it's impossible. Something's not right.

A: No: same birthday, same mother, same name.

B: I suppose there [6]_____ (be) two mothers who were sisters ...

A: No. Same mother. One mother.

B: This is only a possibility ... they [7]_____ (be born) a year apart, so they had the same birthday, but were one year apart.

A: No, it was the same year. Just minutes apart. But ... they had a sister.

B: Oh ... so they [8]_____ (be) triplets!

GRAMMAR relative clauses

6 Complete the article with *who, which, whom, whose* or *when*.

Chinese superstar Lang Lang, [1]_____ has inspired millions of young pianists and [2]_____ performance was a highlight of the opening ceremony of the Beijing Olympics, was born in Shenyang in 1982. From the age of two, [3]_____ his parents paid half a year's salary to buy him a piano, he was brought up to become the world's number one pianist. Lang Lang, [4]_____ was naturally talented, won his first competition at five [5]_____ he had to stand up to play the piano because his feet couldn't reach the pedals. His father, [6]_____ gave up his job as a police officer, moved with him to Beijing for further studies, during [7]_____ time father and son lived in poverty.

Nowadays, he is a young man for [8]_____ playing the piano and being a superstar both come naturally. Lang Lang, [9]_____ work as a Unicef ambassador is dear to his heart, has recently launched a piano competition for children, [10]_____ is sure to be a great success.

FUNCTION reporting an incident

7 Underline the correct alternative.

A: So you let her in your door because she wanted a glass of water?

B: It just didn't [1]*cross/occur/seem* my mind that she was lying.

A: What, a complete stranger coming into your house?

B: She [2]*occurred/seemed/reminded* like a nice person.

A: Didn't you see her pick up your mobile?

B: Well it all happened [3]*such/with/so* fast, but maybe yes.

A: So you saw it but didn't pay attention?

B: Yes. It was only [4]*time/much/immediately* later that I realised what had happened.

A: How old was she would you say?

B: She looked [5]*as/about/like* she was about forty years old.

A: Can you describe her appearance?

B: She [6]*reminded/remembered/looked* me of that actress ...

A: Which one?

B: I don't recall, my mind's gone [7]*blink/blind/blank*.

A: Did she introduce herself?

B: I didn't [8]*cross/grab/catch* her name. It was probably false anyway.

VOCABULARY PLUS dependent prepositions

8 Complete the second sentence so that it has a similar meaning to the first. Use between two and five words including the word given.

1 He said he was sorry because he hadn't listened to her.
   APOLOGISED
   He _____ to her.

2 People think that the website encourages bad behaviour.
   BLAME
   People _____ bad behaviour.

3 TV companies will no longer be allowed to show adverts for fattening foods before 9a.m.
   BANNED
   TV companies will _____ adverts for fattening foods before 9a.m.

4 Because of his quick reactions the plane didn't crash.
   SAVED
   His quick reactions _____ .

5 When children do well, don't forget to praise them.
   PRAISE
   Remember _____ well.

6 Kelly always wanted to be an astronaut.
   DREAMT
   Kelly always _____ an astronaut.

7 The police think Jim helped the robbers escape.
   SUSPECTED
   Jim _____ the robbers escape.

8 She thinks I don't help enough.
   CRITICISING
   She's always _____ enough.

VOCABULARY PLUS two-part phrases

9 Correct the mistake in each two-part phrase.

1 I only wanted peace and ~~downs~~, and what did I get?
   quiet
   A screaming baby!

2 Our relationship has its ups and bounds, but I'd say we're a solid couple.

3 You have to weigh up the leaps and cons, and then decide.

4 There's some back and take in every friendship; don't be so selfish.

5 I'm sick and smooth of your complaints. Shut up or leave!

6 We could go off and on about this forever, let's just end the conversation now.

7 We only meet rough and then, but that's enough for me.

8 Our business was going nowhere, now it's improving in leaps and don'ts.

FUNCTION giving a tour

10A Add vowels to complete the words in the boxes. The words are from functional phrases for giving a tour.

h e a d o v e r	w __ rth
m __ d __ ll __ d	__ pp __ r __ ntly
b __ rnt	m __ y kn __ w

Tour of Kyoto, Japan, part 1

The original city of Kyoto was
1 _____ on the ancient Chinese capital Chang'an. Many buildings were
2 _____ down in the 15th-century Onin war, but the city survived World War II.

As you 3 _____ , Kyoto is famous for its geisha. 4 _____ , women who train to be geisha today are not allowed to marry or have mobile phones. The two famous geisha districts, Gion and Pontocho, are well 5 _____ a visit, so let's 6 _____ there later.

n __ m __ d	r __ tr __ c __
b __ l __ __ v __	
s __ pp __ s __ dly	
f __ __ nd __ d	st __ ry g __ __ s

Tour of Kyoto, Japan, part 2

Here we are at the Jishu shrine. See those two stones? The 7 _____ that if you walk from one to the other, you will one day find true love.

And this is Kiyomizu-dera temple, which was 8 _____ in 798. It's
9 _____ after a waterfall nearby.
10 _____ it or not, not one nail was used to build it.

Why don't we 11 _____ our steps to the Manga Museum –
12 _____ they have over 200,000 titles and we can read as many manga as we want.

B Complete each tour with words from the box above it.

TEST

Circle the correct option to complete the sentences.

1 Her performance was _____ , but otherwise the play was rather _____ .

   a) electrifying, weak   b) chilling, poignant
   c) touching, moving

2 That's strange, I remember _____ this letter, but here it is in my bag.

   a) post   b) posting   c) to post

3 He was _____ for making a serious financial error.

   a) suspected   b) arrested   c) saved

4 My best _____ lives in Paris, works in advertising.

   a) friend who   b) friend, that   c) friend, who

5 There was so much _____ about the new show that it was sure to be a _____ .

   a) hype, letdown   b) rave reviews, flop
   c) ground-breaking, sell-out

6 Your son seems like a future _____ – he loves playing with fire!

   a) hacker   b) mugger   c) arsonist

7 He _____ committed the murder. He wasn't even in the country at the time.

   a) may have   b) can't have   c) mustn't have

8 They'll need to _____ the bridge if taller boats are going to fit under it.

   a) raise   b) deepen   c) broaden

9 It didn't _____ my mind to phone you.

   a) catch   b) occur to   c) cross

10 She was keen to _____ her husband of the crime.

   a) clear   b) blame   c) save

11 I can't believe you _____ that guy who was _____ a tourist.

   a) deceived, snatching   b) were taken in, posing as
   c) were fooled by, pretending to be

12 That's the woman _____ son punched my son.

   a) who   b) whose   c) who's

13 Here we are at the president's childhood home. _____ it's got two floors, and all the other houses around here have one.

   a) Interestingly   b) Supposedly   c) Apparently

14 I think it wouldn't have been a _____ if it hadn't created such a _____ .

   a) must-see, mainstream   b) sell-out, stir
   c) flop, ground-breaking

15 She took her umbrella, _____ that it would rain at some point during the day.

   a) expected   b) expecting   c) having expected

16 The monument was modelled _____ a well-known ancient Egyptian obelisk.

   a) by   b) for   c) after

17 People _____ redundant by the economic crisis were happy to get any kind of job.

   a) make   b) made   c) making

18 The protestors were _____ from marching through the city centre without permission.

   a) accused   b) charged   c) banned

19 I really didn't hear you ring the doorbell. I _____ been sleeping, or maybe I was listening to music.

   a) could have   b) can't have   c) mightn't have

20 They seemed _____ if they were just having fun.

   a) to be   b) like   c) as

21 He _____ my wallet and _____ it for an identical one, which he gave back to me.

   a) grabbed, switched   b) swapped, snatched
   c) fooled, posed

22 Her first relationship was the one thing _____ she thought more than anything else.

   a) which   b) which about   c) about which

23 My foot got _____ in a hole and I couldn't get it out.

   a) run over   b) stuck   c) locked out

24 Look, footprints! Someone _____ got here before us.

   a) could have   b) might have   c) must have

25 _____ all his life to build his dream house, he decided to travel instead.

   a) Having worked   b) Working   c) Worked

26 A search engine is a good _____ tool for checking spelling.

   a) off and on   b) rough-and-ready   c) now and then

27 We stopped on the way up the mountain _____ a break.

   a) to take   b) taking   c) take

28 The tablet's working and my headache's beginning _____ .

   a) going   b) go   c) to go

29 The book was so _____ that I couldn't stay awake.

   a) moving   b) chilling   c) dull

30 My first girlfriend knew me _____ , and no one has understood me as well since.

   a) through and through   b) off and on
   c) ups and downs

TEST RESULT __/30__

AUDIOSCRIPT

UNIT I Recording I

1 I wonder if you could introduce us to the director.
2 Do you mind me asking how much your camera cost?
3 Would you mind telling me what you do exactly?
4 I'd like to know whether it's really worth upgrading to the new smartphone.
5 Can you tell me which platform the Eurostar train leaves from?
6 What do you think he'll do when he discovers the mistake?

UNIT I Recording 2

A: Do you have a dream? Is there something you've always wanted to do but somehow have never managed to? Well my guest today is the man who can make it all happen, for a price of course, Owen Winters, founder of DreamsRreal.com. Owen, welcome to the programme.
B: Thank you for having me.
A: So tell us, how does DreamsRreal work?
B: OK, well it's quite simple. We help people make their lifelong dream come true – whatever it is.
A: So if I, for instance, have dreamt of being a rock star since I was a teenager, you can help me with that.
B: Yes, that's right. And in fact not long ago we had a client, a woman, who wanted exactly that.
A: And you made her a rock star.
B: Well, we couldn't give her talent …
A: Not that rock stars are always talented.
B: Right, but in talking with her, we worked out that the image she had in her mind was doing a live concert to a huge audience. She wanted to experience the sensation of performing in front of thousands of screaming fans.
A: And so how did you manage that?
B: Well, to be honest, it's a bit like producing a scene in a film. In fact that's my background, I worked as a production manager in the film business for many years, till just a few years ago.
A: That's interesting.
B: Yeah, so in this case, we needed to find a venue, an arena where rock concerts are held, a place we could rent out for an evening. Then we needed a backing band, a crew to set the whole thing up and …
A: And how about the thousands of screaming fans?
B: Well, just like getting extras for a film, it's not that difficult.

A: Did you pay the fans?
B: Some of them, yes. We price up the different parts of the plan, write a budget, give the client the figure, and if they agree to the terms, we go ahead and do it.
A: How much did this rock concert cost?
B: I'm afraid I can't tell you. We don't reveal any financial details.
A: Oh, OK. Well, what other dreams have you made come true recently?
B: Let's see, we've just finished working with a client who wants to fly across the Atlantic Ocean on a supersonic aeroplane.
A: But Concorde no longer flies.
B: No, but we've just found a solution to that, using an air force plane. I can't tell you which air force.
A: Another trade secret.
B: A military secret, actually. And another client wants to pilot a submarine. We've done the Normandy beach landings from the Second World War, with the client as general … we've done dining with a movie star, spending a night inside a pyramid, and lots of make-up jobs.
A: Make-up jobs?
B: Yes, some people – all their life – have been curious about what it's like to be a man or a woman, or a celebrity …
A: And you make them up to look the way they want.
B: That's right. We've recently done a job for a guy who wanted to look like Tom Cruise for a day. Our make-up artist did a brilliant job, but the guy couldn't wait for the day to end.
A: Why was that?
B: Too much attention. He couldn't go anywhere without getting asked for an autograph. We suggested that we provide bodyguards, but he didn't want to pay for that.
A: And have you ever had to say no to a request?
B: Hmm … We never say no to a dream. But sometimes it does take time. One client wanted to fly in space, to be an astronaut. That wasn't possible back when she first requested it. But since then it's become possible for ordinary people to go into space, again for a price, and in fact she's blasting off on the next tourist flight.
A: Incredible. So what do you think has been your most extraordinary request, and …

UNIT I Recording 3

1a/b I'm calling to enquire about a reservation I made.
2a/b I was wondering if that's possible.
3a/b Would there be any chance of getting the same price for the following weekend?
4a/b I'd appreciate it if you could make an exception.
5a/b Would you mind telling me why it's so complicated to change?
6a/b Do you mind me asking what your name is?
7a/b I'd like to speak to your supervisor.

UNIT I Recording 4

A: Eden Gardens Hotel. How can I help you?
B: Hi, I'm calling to enquire about a reservation I made. The booking reference is 6714.
A: OK. How can I help you?
B: I need to change the dates to one week later. I was wondering if that's possible, and how much the change will cost.
A: Let me just check. Ah, it's a two-for-one weekend deal.
B: Yes. Would there be any chance of getting the same price for the following weekend?
A: I'm not sure. Bear with me a minute.
B: I'd appreciate it if you could make an exception.
A: I need to ask my supervisor. Can you just hold on a minute? I'll just see …
B: OK …
A: Sorry to keep you. No, sorry, we can't do that.
B: I've got one more question if I'm not keeping you. Would you mind telling me why it's so complicated to change?
A: Sorry, it's policy. Online special deals are non-refundable, non-transferable.
B: Do you mind me asking what your name is then?
A: We aren't allowed to give our full names.
B: In that case, I'd like to speak to your supervisor.

UNIT 2 Recording I

1 She's done all her homework.
She's been doing her homework since she got home from school.
2 I've sent twenty-five application letters this morning.
I've been sending application letters all morning. I need a break!
3 Pete's called and left you a message.
Pete's been calling you all evening. Is your mobile on?

4 I've read this magazine. Do you want to borrow it?

I've been reading this magazine. Do you want to borrow it when I've finished?

5 Julia's gone to the gym – shall I ask her to call you back?

Julia's been going to the gym, and she's ten kilos lighter now.

6 The temperature has dropped to minus thirty.

The temperature has been dropping all day.

UNIT 2 Recording 2

pollution, famine, homelessness, obesity, drug abuse, drunkenness, divorce, drought, debt, domestic violence, poverty, lack of drinking water

UNIT 2 Recording 3

1

I decided to do this because I hate it when people forget my name, like at school the teachers who don't know your name, they don't give you so much attention. So anyway, I looked on some websites to find out the best way to do it. Apparently there are two important things, first is that when you're introduced you really pay attention and look at the person and try to find a way to remember the name. For example, I recently met a woman called Keira and she had curly hair, so Keira, curly, sounds similar, you see what I mean. That was easy. Then secondly you need to repeat the name as often as possible, say it to yourself several times and use it when you're talking to the person. You just have to be careful that you don't sound really strange. Anyway, the result's been good. Somehow people seem friendlier and I feel a lot more confident about chatting to people. The only problem is someone told me it made people uncomfortable because they couldn't remember my name!

2

It was quite difficult at first ... I mean you actually have to stop people trying to give you one; I didn't realise before I started how many are given out all the time. I thought this was a good thing to do because apparently it can take up to a thousand years for one to decay and about thirteen billion are given out each year in the UK alone. And it's not only the pollution but animals and fish can get caught in them. Anyway, I invested in two shopping bags and I've been using them for the past three months. The only problem is I keep forgetting to take them out of the house or I leave them in the car, which is very annoying. My solution has been to get one of those fold-up bags that you can carry in your pocket or bag. I've got all my friends to do the same

and now our local shops are going to become a plastic-bag-free zone. At least that will make me remember to take a bag!

3

I thought this was a good one to try because everyone always looks so bored or miserable, especially on public transport. So the next time I was sitting on a train and someone sat opposite me I looked up and gave them a big smile. They looked a bit surprised but smiled back at me, then buried their face in the newspaper. I got the impression they were a bit embarrassed. Anyway, I continued and kept smiling at all sorts of people during the day. To be honest, I got a mixed reaction, but the kids and older people seemed the friendliest. Oh and I found out later that one woman in the office thought I was flirting with her!

4

I decided to combine two of the ideas. I've always been hopeless at telling jokes, I'm sure it's not because I don't have a sense of humour. It's something about the timing. And I know that jokes are great for building relationships and good for me personally as I often have to give business presentations and a funny story really helps build rapport with the audience. One of the best things about doing this was that I asked all my friends to tell me their favourite jokes and we had lots of laugh-out-loud times together. And I'm getting better, though I did have one very embarrassing moment at work when I told my joke to my boss and he just stared at me like I was an idiot. You want to hear a joke? Something short? OK ... uh, What do cows do on Saturday night? They rent moooovies!

UNIT 2 Recording 4

A: Do you think students should be allowed to use their phones in class?

B: Yeah, I'm in favour of that. The way I see it is that students would be more motivated if they could use phones, maybe to make short movies or things like that.

A: OK, you've got a point there, but you know how kids are. It seems to me that they'd just start texting each other whenever they were bored.

B: I agree to some extent. They would certainly need very strict rules, you know, about turning them on and off. But phones could be useful for things like practising languages or setting homework reminders.

A: Yes, I suppose so, but what about bullying, you know, kids sending each other nasty messages? Or phones could be a target for thieves.

B: Fair enough, but either of those things could happen after school.

A: Hmm. I see your point, but I'm still not convinced. I think on balance it's better to keep them out of classes.

B: I disagree. I think we should encourage them.

UNIT 2 Recording 5

I'm in favour of that.
The way I see it ...
You've got a point there.
It seems to me ...
I agree to some extent ...
I suppose so.
Fair enough, but ...
I see your point, but ...
I'm still not convinced.
I disagree.

UNIT 2 Recording 6

illegal, sensible, unethical, justifiable, inevitable, disturbing, outrageous, inoffensive

RC1 Recording 1

1 drought, exhausted, awkward
2 violence, famine, excited
3 obesity, invasion, matinée
4 illegal, sensible, microchip
5 non-refundable, drug abuse, justifiable

RC1 Recording 2

A group of rock stars are appealing for sponsors to fund a new project aimed at preventing malaria. Recent medical research shows there is a dramatic decrease in the disease when malaria nets are provided for families.

Fifty-two tourists have been rescued from the desert near the Step Pyramid in Egypt after temperatures reached 49 degrees Celsius – the highest level ever recorded in the area. The tourists were stranded when their bus broke down. The group's tour operator has been arrested for failing to obtain a permit to conduct business in the area.

And in business, a number of European countries are planning to cut imports from the United States as trade tensions continue. The USA has recently increased taxes on all goods coming from abroad to an all-time high.

UNIT 3 Recording 1

1

I'm logged on twenty-four hours a day, and each time a message comes in I check it ... I start getting frustrated if I don't get at least one an hour. Nowadays, I often don't answer the phone when my old friends call. Almost all my friends are people I've met online – the other day I met some people I knew from uni and I actually found it quite strange talking to them face to face because I'm much more used to interacting with people online. I'm a bit worried because my eyes are starting to hurt real bad ...

2

It's the quizzes and other applications that get me, like there's always a new questionnaire or test for something, you know, 'Do your friends think you're cool?' or 'How long would you survive on a desert island?' Then there's Farmville, you know, where you have to manage a farm – I've been doing that for the last two months. Now I can't stop thinking about it, I lie in bed at night planning what I'll do when I log on next time. So of course, I'm not ...

3

When I was in high school I was completely hooked. I used to sit in lessons checking my texts, and sometimes I told the teacher I was ill so I could go outside and log on to chat with friends. I would often skip lunch so I could carry on chatting. I spent more time online than I did studying so then my grades went down ...

4

I realised it was getting ridiculous when my daughter actually sent me a message through Facebook asking for help with her homework ... I mean, she was only in the next room! To be fair, she probably asked me in person first but I suppose I'd got so absorbed in the site that I didn't hear her. I'm also not taking proper care of myself – I have terrible headaches all the time. I know you're supposed to stop and give yourself a break regularly, but I never remember. Anyway, after that ...

5

I lost my job because of it. It started out that I'd just go onto the website during coffee breaks, but then I started to log on during work time. When a chat message came in, I couldn't resist, I'd stop what I was doing and join the conversation ... and my boss noticed that I was working less and less. He warned me a couple of times ... then he fired me. So then I ...

UNIT 3 Recording 2

1 I used to <u>love</u> it.
2 I didn't use to <u>discuss</u> it.
3 We'd always <u>eat</u> together.
4 We'd always <u>argue</u>.
5 He's not <u>used</u> to it yet.
6 I'm getting <u>used</u> to it.
7 She can't get <u>used</u> to it.
8 I've got <u>used</u> to it.

UNIT 3 Recording 3

The way it works is that you draw a grid of 5x5 on a piece of paper. There are two players, and the object of the game is to complete the sequence 'SOS' in a straight line as many times as you can. So the first thing you do is one of you writes an 'S' or an 'O' in one of the squares. Then the other player writes an 'S' or an 'O' in another square. Whenever one of you completes an 'SOS', you get another turn and basically the point is not to let your partner succeed, so what usually happens is that one player gets an 'SOS' and then blocks the other player. It's easy to lose track of who's winning so the key thing is to keep score of who gets how many 'SOSs'. Then after you've finished (once the grid is full), the winner is the player with the most 'SOSs'.

UNIT 3 Recording 4

1 Look up the idiom <u>where</u>?
2 I should see <u>who</u>?
3 You last spoke to her <u>when</u>?
4 I can use a question word to <u>do what</u>?
5 <u>Who's</u> waiting backstage?
6 The rain's doing <u>what</u>?
7 I'll find you <u>where</u>?
8 The <u>what's</u> too high?

UNIT 4 Recording 1

An eight-year-old boy has been rescued by an enterprising Bangkok firefighter.

The boy from Thailand is autistic and had been feeling very nervous before his first day of school but initially he seemed to be OK. However, during the first lesson his teacher was explaining something to the class when she realised that the boy had climbed out of the window. 'He was sitting just outside the window with his legs swinging over the edge.'

The rescue services were called in when the boy's mother had also failed to get the boy down. Everyone was beginning to run out of ideas when one of the firefighters, Somchai Yoosabai, overheard the boy's mother talking about her son's love of superheroes. The quick-thinking fireman rushed back to the fire station and changed into his Spider-Man costume. Until then, Mr Somchai had been using the costume to make school fire drills more interesting. 'I told him "Spider-Man is here to rescue you, no monsters are going to attack you." ' The sight brought a smile to the youngster's face and he immediately walked into his rescuer's arms.

UNIT 4 Recording 2

Hello and welcome to Arts Review. In tonight's programme we look at a rather surprising answer to the question: How many stories exist? You might think that there are hundreds or thousands of different stories in literature, theatre and film but experts like to put the number rather lower, anything between one and twelve. Now, in a new book, Christopher Booker says that there are exactly seven basic 'plots' and every story in the world can fit into one of them. Before we review his book, here are the seven:

Plot one: Overcoming the monster.

In this story, the hero or heroine has to battle and defeat a monster. This could be a real monster for example, Dracula, or it could be a person, such as a villain in a James Bond film. The monster is defeated, the hero is victorious, the community is saved and order returns to the world. Most detective stories are actually variations on the theme of overcoming the monster.

Plot two: Rags to riches.

This idea is found in countless stories. It involves a very ordinary person or someone that everyone thinks is normal, nothing special. Then during the course of the story, it's shown that this person is in fact extraordinary. Just think of the story of Superman or any story of an ordinary person who ends up marrying someone rich.

Plot three: The quest.

This features a main character who travels a long distance, often with companions, in search of a treasure or to do a brave or noble act. At the end he or she succeeds and is rewarded in some way, often by keeping the treasure or sometimes by saving a community. Probably the best known example of this is *The Lord of the Rings*. Interestingly, it's also often the basis of many computer games.

Plot four: Voyage and return.

This typically tells the story of an ordinary person who is thrown into a completely strange and alien world, one that is outside their experience. Often they face dangers and difficulties and then have a thrilling escape back to their original situation. There was a TV series called *Lost* about people whose plane crashed on a desert island. That was a voyage and return story.

Plot five: Comedy.

This doesn't always mean humour although the story can be funny. It's more about a situation which is full of mistakes and mix-ups. The whole story gets more and more confused until at the end everything is sorted out and there's a happy ending.

Plot six: Tragedy.

As its name suggests, this plot never has a happy ending. It's about what terrible things can happen when someone tries to get power or go against the system … this person often has a weakness in their character and this weakness is the reason that everything ends badly. There are lots of examples in theatre, such as Romeo and Juliet, who fall in love although their families hate each other.

Plot seven: Rebirth.

This plot is about a person in a dark and difficult situation, maybe they've lost all their money or their job or they are in prison. Or perhaps he or she is unpopular or has an unpleasant personality. Then a series of events happens, often amazing events, and the situation or the person changes so that the character becomes a kind of hero, a very positive character.

So that's all seven. Before we go onto discuss these, there's an interesting quote from the American novelist, Kurt Vonnegut, who claimed …

UNIT 4 Recording 3

1 I wish I'd had more money.
2 I wish you'd worked harder at school.
3 I wish it would stop raining.
4 I shouldn't have told her.
5 We should have gone to the party.
6 You shouldn't have turned it off.

UNIT 4 Recording 4

A: What did you think of the book?
B: Well, I'm not a big fan of travel books.
A: Oh, why's that?
B: I'm not that keen on all the description.

A: I hear Nick's enjoying his new school.
B: Yes, what he loves about it is that they do a lot of sport.
A: I didn't know he liked sport.
B: Oh, yeah. He's really into football at the moment.

A: Why don't you like barbecues?
B: I can't stand it when the meat isn't cooked properly.
A: You haven't tasted *my* barbecues!
B: And the other thing I hate about them is the mosquitoes.
A: OK. Maybe we'd better stay inside.

UNIT 4 Recording 5

1 Well, I'm not a big <u>fan</u> of <u>travel</u> <u>books</u>.
2 I'm not <u>that</u> <u>keen</u> on all the <u>description</u>.
3 <u>Yes</u>, what he <u>loves</u> about it is they do a lot of <u>sport</u>.
4 Oh, <u>yeah</u>. He's <u>really</u> into <u>football</u> at the <u>moment</u>.
5 I can't <u>stand</u> it when the <u>meat</u> isn't <u>cooked</u> <u>properly</u>.
6 And the <u>other</u> <u>thing</u> I <u>hate</u> about them is the <u>mosquitoes</u>.

RC2 Recording 1

1 biography, hindsight, proximity
2 criticise, sieve, lyrics
3 ignore, autobiography, cloud
4 generous, summit, double-click
5 encyclopedia, pity, lean
6 opportunity, stubborn, forested

UNIT 5 Recording 1

A: Have you ever wondered why pregnant women don't tip over? Why woodpeckers don't get headaches? Or why, if you bend a piece of dry spaghetti, it often breaks into three or more pieces? Well, researchers have studied questions like these, and some of these researchers have received the so-called Ig Nobel Prize for their work. And here to talk to us about the Prize is Martha Anton. So Martha, what is the Ig Nobel prize and what's your connection to it?
B: Well, the name of the prize is of course a play on words – it's not the Nobel, it's the Ig-Nobel, as in *ignoble* – and it's awarded to researchers and inventors for doing work which first makes you laugh, then makes you think.
A: So it's not a serious award.
B: Well, yes and no. Sometimes it's given to someone as a criticism of their work, sometimes as a point of humour, but in many cases the prize goes to someone for doing something that we might think is really silly or trivial, but which might lead to a major breakthrough. Some of the most important discoveries in history started with a joke. And at the awards ceremony, actual winners of the Nobel Prize present the Ig Nobel Prizes.
A: And what's your connection with the Ig Nobel Prize?
B: Besides the fact that I've always been a big fan of the prize and fascinated by the sort of people who win it, I'm hoping to win it myself.
A: I'd like to ask you about that in a minute. So what other research has won the Ig Nobel?
B: Well, two researchers in Newcastle won the Veterinary Medicine prize for showing that if you give a cow a name, and use the name, it will give more milk.
A: Fascinating.
B: And there have been a great many inventions, for example a teenager repellent.
A: A teenager repellent?
B: Yes, it's a device that makes an annoying noise that only teenagers can hear.
A: So adults can use it to keep teenagers away.

B: That's right.
A: I can't imagine why they'd want to do that.
B: Well, actually it was developed and it's been used by shopkeepers who want to stop teenagers hanging around outside their shops.
A: Really?
B: And then there's the alarm clock that runs away and hides. So that people can't switch it off and go back to sleep.
A: Incredible!
B: That won the Ig Nobel for Economics, because it helps add more work hours to the day.
A: Naturally.
B: Oh yes, some years ago two Japanese researchers won the prize for their device called the Bow-Lingual. It translates from dog talk to human talk.
A: The Bow-Lingual. I get it.
B: And a Korean won for inventing a business suit that automatically perfumes itself.
A: So that a businessperson doesn't walk into a meeting smelling bad.
B: My favourite though was the washing machine for dogs and cats.
A: That would work perfectly with the Bow-Lingual. So what is your invention?
B: It's research actually, into whether it's better to walk or run in the rain. If you don't have an umbrella, that is.
A: Hm. Which way you get less wet, you mean.
B: Yes that's right.
A: And so which is better?
B: Ummm … I'm afraid we haven't finished the research yet. Give me another six months of bad weather and we'll have the answer!

UNIT 5 Recording 2 ~TRACK 25~

detrimental, beneficial, revolutionise, enhance, distort, transform, damage, alter

UNIT 5 Recording 3 TRACK 26

A: What do you think about simply writing the rule on a sign on the wall: 'English only?'

B: I think it's too simple. We would ignore it.

C: How do you feel about a fine system? You have to pay if you speak your language.

B: That's not original enough.

A: Suppose we try a mother-tongue 'island.' A place in the room where you can go to speak your mother tongue if you really need to.

C: That's a terrific idea.

B: It doesn't grab me.

A: Would you consider having five-minute mother-tongue breaks in the middle of the lesson?

B: I think we're on the wrong track here. It's either punishment or reward, nothing else works.

C: How does giving a prize for using only English strike you? Like no homework? Or chocolate?

B: I'd go for that.

A: It'd be great if we could get more different nationalities in the group. Then we'd naturally speak English more.

B: That's not very realistic.

C: I'm torn between punishment and reward systems. Fines or prizes.

A: Could we go for both?

B: Yeah, let's go with that.

UNIT 5 Recording 4 TRACK 27

1 With respect, we need to be more focussed.

2 To be honest, I thought your first suggestion was better.

3 To put it bluntly, that's the worst idea I've heard today.

4 Actually, I don't think that's a very practical idea.

5 Frankly, it's just not going to work.

6 As a matter of fact, that's probably the only way.

UNIT 5 Recording 5

1 obscure
2 predictable
3 absurd
4 ambitious
5 weird
6 dreadful
7 unrealistic
8 brilliant

UNIT 6 Recording 1

1

I don't think there's any hard and fast rule, so for me, any time is the right time. I began when I was six, but then again I knew someone who started when they were almost fifty and she's still going strong now she's over seventy. You're never too old. I suppose the key is how much time you have to practise and your motivation. My parents let me try out different instruments and eventually I chose the violin. That's important too. I'm not sure my parents were too happy about my choice, though! They had to put up with years of me sounding like a dying cat!

2

I think there's actually a legal minimum age in some countries, something like thirty-five, but in my opinion it should be at least fifty. Otherwise you just don't have enough experience to do it. But then of course you have to strike a balance between maturity and energy. You need to be able to react quickly to events and survive sometimes on very little sleep. So yes, someone in their fifties or maybe sixties could manage but no older than that.

3

I couldn't really give a number at all, since I can't state what's right for other people ... I think it has to do with giving yourself enough time to get to know yourself, and to understand your relationship together well enough so that neither of you will create an unhealthy environment for the child. Some people say there's never a right time, but I think there's definitely a wrong time – too soon.

4

Lots of people I know didn't know what they wanted to do with their life when they were twenty and they still don't know now they're over forty! But seriously, it's OK to decide young, if you have a real vocation, you know, you've always wanted to be a doctor or an engineer or something like that. But most of us don't have much idea when we leave school. So I reckon the best idea is to try out lots of things to see what you enjoy and develop lots of general skills. That worked for me. Most companies need staff who can get on with other people and can communicate their ideas clearly, and who have reasonable computer skills and things like that.

UNIT 6 Recording 2

/ɪ/, little:	enjoy, pretence, prefer, encourage
/iː/, eat:	appreciate, achievement
/aɪ/, sky:	oblige, advise
/e/, red:	preference

UNIT 6 Recording 3

1

A: Look at this picture. Isn't it time that they banned 'size zero' models?

B: Well, clothes do look quite good on them.

A: Doesn't it matter to you that young girls think it's normal to be so skinny?

B: I've never really thought about it much.

A: Well you should. Clearly it's not right.

B: Yeah, I'm sure you're right.

2

A: Don't you think that they should use technology in football games?

B: What, you mean instead of referees?

A: Yeah, to make decisions. Anyone can see it would be fairer.

B: But you need referees for all sorts of reasons.

A: Yeah, but surely it's more important that decisions are correct.

B: Hmm. I suppose you have a point.

UNIT 6 Recording 4

1

A: Do you like me in this dress?

B: I prefer the white one.

A: So what you're saying is that this one, which cost a fortune, looks terrible.

B: No, I mean the white one makes you look slimmer.

A: So in other words I look fat!

B: No, no, you're twisting my words. I just meant that you look *even* slimmer in the white one.

2

A: Don't you think we should pay a decorator to do it?

B: What you're getting at is you don't think I can do it.

A: I didn't mean that. It's just that it might be quicker and save us money.

B: So I gather your point is that I might mess it up.

A: No, but you're a perfectionist and you know how long it takes you to do things.

B: So if I've got it right, you'd rather spend money and end up with a worse job!

A: Not exactly ...

RC3 Recording 1

1 damage, promising, advertise
2 beneficial, achieve, revolutionise
3 ambitious, predictable, maturity
4 wear, weird, interference
5 dreadful, pretend, appreciate
6 campaign, reaction, breakthrough

UNIT 7 Recording 1

1

One of my favourite programmes when I was a kid was a very famous show called *Mister Ben*. I don't really remember that much about it, I know it was my favourite because my mother tells me it was. It was a cartoon, and from what I remember it's about a guy who goes into a fancy clothes shop and he puts on a different outfit and then every time he comes out of the clothes shop he's then transported to a world that corresponds with the outfit that he's wearing. I think I liked it because there was this innocent sense of adventure about it. I can't remember much about any individual episodes though.

2

The classic for Brits of my generation is *Blue Peter* – it's hard to underestimate its cultural impact. It was a kind of magazine programme for children. Basically, it involved two or three presenters (who also had a dog and a cat) involved in various tasks – demonstrating how to make toys or ornaments out of everyday household objects, short documentary trips to various places of interest and so on. Occasionally they held interviews with famous actors or performers of some sort. They would also bring in people who had some form of talent – musical, for example – to do live studio performances. Everyone wanted a 'Blue Peter badge', the special prize you could be awarded if you wrote in and they read your letter, or if you won a competition or something similar – literally a badge of honour.

3

I liked this show *Grange Hill* because it was I think an accurate representation of what life in an English comprehensive school in a British city is like and it dealt with issues that were interesting for teen ... perhaps a bit younger than teenagers ... So like when you were from nine to twelve. I think it was a really good show because you're not yet old enough to watch adult TV but you're too old to watch kids' TV and it kind of bridges the gap between the two, and it deals with issues like drugs and sex in an unpatronising, uncondescending way. I suppose it was a kind of soap opera for kids, but quite a serious one.

4

When I was a teenager, my favourite show was *Monty Python*. It was different from any other kind of comedy show we'd had before. Instead of separate sketches with proper endings, in *Monty Python* they'd start a sketch and then suddenly stop it halfway or one sketch would morph into another. If a sketch was getting boring there'd be a news announcer coming on and saying 'and now for something completely different!' The links between the sketches would sometimes be cartoons, very surrealistic and weird cartoons of people exploding or strange machines. I suppose one of the main reasons I liked it was because my parents didn't understand it at all, so it was a kind of rebellion. After a Monty Python night we'd spend our entire lunch break at school going through it, remembering all the catchphrases and taking each sketch apart.

UNIT 7 Recording 2

1 If I say something offensive, I'm often too stubborn to take it <u>back</u>.
2 I can put <u>up</u> with a noisy hotel room more than a dirty one.
3 If someone's car breaks <u>down</u>, I know how to fix it.
4 Hard work brings <u>out</u> the best in me.
5 I come <u>across</u> as being more sociable than I really am.
6 If it turned <u>out</u> that my partner had lied to me, I would be disappointed in him.
7 If I locked my keys in my car, I would simply break <u>into</u> it.
8 When I agree to do something, I never pull <u>out</u> even if I feel ill.

UNIT 7 Recording 3

A: This is totally <u>ridiculous</u>. Where are my <u>keys</u>? The <u>annoying</u> thing is that I had them a <u>minute</u> ago. Oh, it <u>does</u> make me <u>so</u> mad when I can't <u>find</u> them!
B: Well, <u>you're</u> the one who's always <u>telling</u> me to put them somewhere <u>safe</u>. Have you tried the <u>door</u>?
A: There's <u>no way</u> I'd leave them <u>there</u>!
B: Okay, I'm just trying to <u>help</u>. There's no need to get into such a <u>state</u>!
A: I'm <u>not</u> 'in a <u>state</u>'. Now where on <u>earth</u> did I last have them?

UNIT 8 Recording 1

1 What would <u>you</u> have <u>done</u>?
2 I <u>wouldn't</u> have done <u>that</u>.
3 If I'd <u>known</u> when you were <u>coming</u>, I would've <u>met</u> you at the <u>station</u>.

UNIT 8 Recording 2

Part 1

Today, in the third of my lectures on human behaviour, I'm going to talk about the difference between the way people act when they're being watched – or think they're being watched – and how they act when they're unobserved. I'll be describing a recent experiment conducted at Newcastle University. I'll be drawing conclusions from this experiment, to see what it teaches us about psychology and behaviour and finally, I'll be comparing it with other key research findings in the area.

So, what did the team at Newcastle set out to discover? They wanted to find out whether the simple belief that they were being watched would alter people's behaviour. To do this they made use of an 'honesty box' in a staff common room at the university. The idea behind the 'honesty box' was that staff members would pay the correct amount for their coffee and tea. This honesty box had been in there for several years, so no one had any idea that an experiment was taking place. What they did was to place a small poster at eye-level above the honesty box, listing the prices for the drinks. However, each week the poster alternated between different images of either flowers or of a pair of eyes looking straight at the observer. Here, you can see examples of the kind of pictures they used. At the end of each week the team monitored the amount of money that had been collected and compared this to the volume of milk that had been consumed. They found that people paid nearly three times as much money when the notice included a pair of eyes as when it included an image of flowers.

UNIT 8 Recording 3

Part 2

So what does this experiment tell us? Well, firstly it underlines something we already know – that our brains are hard-wired, are programmed, to respond to faces and eyes. It's important for people to know if they're being watched. Secondly, it shows that people are influenced if they think they're being watched; they behave less selfishly. The team were surprised by the significant difference in the findings.

And what implications could this have for the future? Well, the team believe the idea could be applied to public situations where people have to decide whether to behave well or badly. One example would be for warnings for speed cameras. The team's previous studies show that drivers would react more positively to images of faces and eyes than to a picture of a camera. Another place where a picture of eyes could be placed is near a CCTV camera in town centres.

Now, before I go on to discuss other studies, does anyone have any questions?

UNIT 8 Recording 4

A: Is everything OK?

B: Actually, there's something I've been meaning to talk to you about.

A: Oh, is there a problem?

B: I don't want you to get the wrong idea, but …

A: That sounds bad.

B: It's just that you often leave your mobile on.

A: I don't understand.

B: And it rings when you're not here, and that's annoying.

A: But I need to keep it on in case my son phones.

B: Yes, but it's disturbing when people are trying to work.

A: It's important that he can get straight through to me.

B: I understand, but do you see where I'm coming from?

A: I suppose so.

B: Maybe you could set it to silent when you're not here.

A: What you mean just the 'vibrate' setting?

B: Yes, how would you feel about that?

A: OK, that sounds reasonable. I'll do that from now on. Sorry about that.

B: Thanks, I'd appreciate it.

UNIT 8 Recording 5

1 Actually, there's something I've um been meaning to talk to you about.

2 Well, I don't want you to get the wrong idea, but …

3 It's just that you know you often leave your mobile on …

4 And it rings when you're not here and that's slightly annoying.

5 Yes, but it's a bit disturbing when people are trying to work.

6 I understand, but I mean, do you see where I'm coming from?

7 Maybe you could just set it to silent when you're not here.

8 Yes, how would you er feel about that?

RC4 Recording 1

1 biased, deny, promise

2 reality, threaten, dread

3 serial, circulation, alert

4 persuade, tabloid, sensationalist

5 focussed, confrontational, colourful

6 sensible, aggressive, despise

UNIT 9 Recording 1

A: … and we're joined today by Alex Temple, a researcher in something called inattentional blindness. Welcome to the show.

B: Thank you.

A: So for starters, can you tell us exactly what is 'inattentional blindness'?

B: Well the best way I can explain it is through some of the experiments that have been done. The most famous is the gorilla experiment. Subjects are shown a film of two groups throwing around a basketball, one group dressed in white, the other in dark clothes. And the viewer is told to count the number of times the team in white passes the ball. After about ten seconds, someone dressed in a gorilla suit walks out to the middle, faces the camera and then walks off. Most people watching the film don't notice the gorilla.

A: Don't notice it? That's hard to believe.

B: It seems that way till you do it. The point is that it's part of the nature of how we see, or don't see, when we pay attention.

A: You mean when we pay attention we see less.

B: When we pay attention we see what we're paying attention to. If I ask you to go out on Oxford Street and count the number of people with glasses, then when you come back I ask how many teenagers you saw with parrots on their shoulders, we'd get a similar result, even if there were several teenagers with parrots.

A: I suppose so. But why is this so important?

UNIT 9 Recording 2

B: Well, when this happens in everyday life it can have significant consequences – a lot of accidents happen because of inattentional blindness.

A: For example?

B: Well, for example road accidents. Many accidents happen when a driver is talking on his or her mobile phone, using a hands-free set-up, which is legal. A driver in this situation actually misses a great deal of visual information, or is slower to process it.

A: A car stopping in front of them for instance?

B: Exactly. When there's a smooth flow of traffic, and the driver is talking on the phone, some of their ability to process visual information is taken away. A car stops in front of them and it's like the gorilla – it's not what they're concentrating on, or looking for, and so they don't 'see' it. They also tend not to notice advertising hoardings by the road, for instance, even quite striking ones.

A: Maybe this explains why I miss signs when I'm driving.

B: Well, if you're driving in the USA and you're looking for a sign that says 'city centre' you might not notice the one that says 'downtown'. Even if you're not talking on the phone. That's more about selective seeing, which is related to inattentional blindness.

A: And how is this … information used?

B: In lots of ways. We use simulators to demonstrate to trained pilots that they're less likely to notice something unusual on the airport runway than an untrained person – and this awareness helps them adjust how they use their visual perception and processing, and can prevent accidents.

A: Fascinating.

B: And in more common jobs, like a guard in a store. They expect a thief to try and hide what they're doing, so if someone steals something openly – just smiles, greets the guard, and walks out of the store – they might not notice it. We do simulations to train guards not to be blinded by their expectations of how a thief behaves.

A: So it's really about training people not to be blind.

B: Yes. Though we've seen applications in design too. It's happened that a car driver driving at night tried to overtake another car and simply didn't see the motorcycle coming in the other direction – because the headlights didn't look like car headlights. So some motorcycle headlights have been made to look more like car headlights.

A: Any advice for our listeners? Is this something they can use in everyday life?

B: Sure. Aside from not talking on the phone while driving, I'd say that it's important to be aware of how you're looking at things. How your expectations of what you'll see actually blinds you to what's there.

A: So, expect the unexpected?

B: Yes, exactly.

UNIT 9 Recording 3

arson, stalking, vandalism, kidnapping, hacking, shoplifting, mugging, counterfeiting, pickpocketing, tax evasion, bribery, identity theft

UNIT 9 Recording 4

A: I've just been robbed, on the underground. By a pickpocket.

B: What happened?

A: Well, this guy got on the train and he reminded me of that English football player … wait, my mind's gone blank. Oh yeah, David Beckham.

B: David Beckham? Didn't you wonder why he was travelling on the underground?

A: It never occurred to me, no. Well, then everyone crowded round with their phonecams.

B: Typical!

A: I had to push my way past them and before I'd realised what was happening my wallet was gone, right out of my bag.

B: Did you see or feel anyone take it?

A: No, in fact it was only a minute later that I realised they'd done it. It all happened so fast, and I was in a hurry anyway.

B: So the David Beckham lookalike must have been a distraction.

A: Yeah, and he must have had someone working with him.

B: Well, the people with phonecams, maybe they …

A: Do you think? They seemed like students, but …

B: Oh, definitely, it was a pickpocket gang. That's how they work.

UNIT 9 Recording 5

A: It was a pretty bad accident. The front rim was completely twisted.

B: Rim?

A: The metal part of the wheel. And of course the spokes were broken.

B: Spokes?

A: The wires that go from the centre of the wheel to the rim. The chain guard got dented.

B: Chain guard?

A: The metal thing that covers the chain. One pedal broke off.

B: Pedal?

A: The thing you put your foot in. And the handlebar got bent.

B: Handlebar?

A: The thing you hold when you ride. And somehow the saddle got ripped.

B: Saddle?

A: The thing you sit on when you ride a bike.

B: Oh dear. Did you break any bones?

A: Bones? I cracked my skull.

B: Skull?

A: That's the big bone inside your head …

UNIT 10 Recording 1

1 The people living on the other side of the river were trapped.

2 Anyone planning to go home early or wanting to take a break should let us know.

3 Walking out of the restaurant, I ran into my old boss coming in.

4 I used to work with the woman living next door.

5 I left the party quickly, not telling anyone that I was unwell.

6 Carrying a child under each arm, she ran out of the blazing building.

7 He jumped up, frightened by the loud bang, mistaking the door for a gun.

8 Walls painted white tend to attract more graffiti.

UNIT 10 Recording 2
Part 1

Hello everyone and thank you for coming. This evening I'm going to talk to you about how to take great photographs – the five secrets that every good photographer knows and uses. To be honest, these aren't really 'secrets,' but hopefully, they'll be new to some of you and you'll find them useful.

OK, let's start with a photograph that includes some of the most common basic mistakes that amateurs make … As you can see, this photo is a typical snapshot, the sort where someone got the woman to pose for the camera. Nothing against posing, though my preference is for more natural shots, but in any case there are five basic errors.

First of all, the picture-taker made sure the sun was behind him or her, to avoid sun going into the lens, and that's good but this way the subject has the sun blasting on her face, just a flat hard light.

Secondly, the head is centred, which leaves all this space at the top and sometimes cuts off the subject's lower body, though that's not the case here.

Thirdly, the background does nothing – it's there, more or less in focus, but it's not interesting in any way, which is a kind of missed opportunity.

Fourthly, overall there's too much space around the subject, the picture taker is either too far away or zoomed out too much or both. This is obviously supposed to be a picture of this woman, but you can hardly see her face, she's simply too small in the frame.

Finally, the angle is odd, though you might not appreciate this until I show you how to improve on it; but basically the camera is at the height of the photographer's eyes, about one and a half metres, looking down on the subject, and the woman is looking up, which is not the best angle to see a face.

You might think I'm being unfair, as this is just a quick snapshot. But I want you to see just how simple it is to make even your family snapshots consistently good photos.

UNIT 10 Recording 3
Part 2

OK, so here are the five key rules:
Rule number one: Light from the side. So if you're outside, notice where the sun is shining from and position yourself so that it's to your left or right as you're facing your subject. If it's to your side, the subject won't have that flat hard light on them, but much more interesting shadows and shades, which give the image more depth and contour.

Rule number two is the rule of thirds. When you're framing a shot, divide the screen up into thirds both horizontally and vertically, and think of the four points where the lines intersect as centres. If your subject is a face, centre the face at one of these four points. As to which one, that is sometimes obvious but it also depends on the background.

Which brings us to rule number three: Think about your background – think of your background as a supporting actor for your subject – and make it work for you. It should be interesting. I know that sounds general, but just think about great paintings – the background is never unimportant. It may mean positioning yourself in a particular way so, for example, there are trees or water or sky behind your subject and not cars.

Rules number four and five are simpler: four is to take three steps closer to your subject. Try to fill the picture with your subject rather than leaving a lot of air around – unless the background or surroundings are important. And rule number five is to adjust your height to your subject, so if they're much shorter, for example a child, kneel or crouch down. The lens and their eyes should be at about the same level. You'll be amazed at the difference.

So those are five rules. Let's look at another photo of the same person and see how the rules work in practice.

UNIT 10 Recording 4

1 It's well worth a visit
2 Let's head over to the
3 Supposedly, they had to interrupt
4 Believe it or not, it took
5 It was originally built as
6 Well, they were founded in
7 Let's retrace our steps to
8 The story goes that he used

RC5 Recording 1

1 rescue, touching, mugging
2 hype, height, chilling
3 poignant, now and then, ground-breaking
4 rave reviews, accuse, dull
5 hacker, cause, fall for
6 electrifying, bribery, deceive

ANSWER KEY

1.1

1A b

B

1 b   2 c   3 a   4 b

C

1 F: Whether that's true is open to debate …

2 T: a professor of journalism

3 F: This evening's event … is free.

4 T: Many of those attending are unwilling to talk about their worries to anyone but the therapists.

5 F: Jones's advice hardly seems original, but Novac says he is satisfied.

6 T: That's actually why many therapists take part in the event, Jones tells us. 'This is a great source of new clients.'

7 F: Some of those seeking advice aren't entirely happy with the format. 'People near me can hear what I'm telling the therapist,' remarks Donna Bersch.

8 F: But with the loud buzz in the room that sometimes reaches the level of shouting … they're lucky to be able to hear the person sitting opposite them!

D

1 format   2 brainchild
3 stumbled across   4 quandaries
5 phobias   6 succinct   7 position
8 eavesdrop

2

1 Why have you come to see me today?

2 What are these headaches like?

3 What causes the/these headaches, do you think?

4 What are you thinking about at the moment?

5 Does that clock remind you of anything?

6 Why's/Why is that?

7 OK. How would you like to pay – in cash or by credit card?

3A

1 wonder if you could introduce

2 asking how much your camera

3 telling me what you

4 whether it's/it is really

5 the Eurostar train leaves

6 think he'll/he will do

4A

1 I don't know why you say he's down-to-earth,

2 I was never **particular** about what I eat,

3 Fabio tends to keep **to** himself and goes to bed very late,

4 My colleague Bill is a real **people** person,

5 He's a good **laugh**, but with money

a) he tends to be **tight-fisted** and never pays.

b) as he does his best work in the early **hours**, when no one's around.

c) so it's odd that he doesn't really **pull** his weight when we work together.

d) I think he's a real computer **geek**, and he's not very practical.

e) but that's changed since I've started getting **into** cooking.

B

1 d   2 e   3 b   4 c   5 a

5A

1 wo   2 v/gr   3 sp   4 gr   5 p   6 st
7 ww

B

1 when you are arriving

2 I'm attaching

3 address

4 quick

5 expensive. From there …

6 need/want

7 give me a call

1.2

1A

1 embarrassing   2 exhausted
3 satisfied   4 thrilled   5 awkward
6 relieved   7 anxious   8 fascinating
9 frustrating   10 impressed

B

1 satisfied   2 exhausted   3 fascinating
4 embarrassing   5 frustrating
6 awkward   7 relieved   8 anxious
9 impressed   10 thrilled

C

1, 4, 5, 6, 7, 8, 9

2A

1 C   2 A   3 B

B

1 c   2 a   3 c   4 b   5 b

C

P: 3 (becoming a rock star; dining with a movie star; looking like a celebrity/Tom Cruise)

T: 3 (flying across the Atlantic on a supersonic aeroplane; piloting a submarine; flying in space/becoming an astronaut)

H: 2 (the Normandy beach landings from the Second World War; spending a night inside a pyramid)

3

1 've/have always wanted, have never managed

2 had, wanted

3 worked

4 did the concert cost, has (the cost) gone

5 have (you) made

6 've/have just finished

7 requested

8 's/has become

4

1 Has, seen, left, went

2 Have, spoken, haven't asked

3 did, get back, 've/have already forgotten, were, happened

4 has had, stayed, had, has been

5A

1 satisfaction   2 Generosity
3 anxiety   4 embarrassment, embarrassment   5 disappointment
6 nervousness   7 similarity
8 awkwardness   9 frustration

B

M: 1   S: 9   A: 2, 3, 4, 5, 6, 7, 8

1.3

1

1 enrolment   2 Sign   3 in
4 refundable   5 matinee   6 served
7 for   8 limited

2

1 I'm calling to enquire about

2 I was wondering if that is/if that's

3 Would there be any chance of getting

4 I'd appreciate it if you could

5 Would you mind **telling** me

6 Do you **mind** me asking what your name is

7 I'd like to speak to

3

1a) P b) 1   2a) 1 b) P   3a) 1 b) P

4a) P b) I 5a) I b) P 6a) P b) I

7a) P b) I

4A

1 I'd really appreciate your help.

2 Sorry to be difficult it's just that ...

3 Bear with me a minute.

4 I've got one more question, if I'm not keeping you.

5 Sorry to keep you.

6 Can you hold on a minute? I'll just see ...

B

1 = 3   2 = 6   3 = 5   4 = 4

UNIT 2

2.1

1A

1 b a, 2 a b, 3 b a, 4 b a, 5 b a,
6 b a

2

1 've/have been travelling

2 've/have visited

3 've/have often wanted

4 've/have never known

5 've/have been exploring

6 've/have found

7 's/has been presenting

8 have told

9 has been

10 has recently appeared

3A

1 pollution   2 famine
3 homelessness   4 obesity
5 drug abuse   6 drunkenness
7 divorce   8 drought   9 debt
10 domestic violence   11 poverty
12 lack of drinking water

C

1/2 drought/debt   3 famine
4 divorce   5/6/7 homelessness/
drunkenness/poverty   8 pollution
9 obesity   10 drug abuse
11 domestic violence
12 lack of drinking water

4A

1 To make the world a better place, by giving people ideas on small actions they can do as individuals.

2 E: 1, 4, 6, 7; PS: 2, 3, 5, 8

B

1=5   2=7   3=2   4=3, 8

C

1a) hates it when people forget her name; particularly at school – teachers don't give you as much attention if they don't know your name

b) makes people uncomfortable because they can't remember her name

2a) pollution – it takes 1,000 years for a plastic bag to decay; animals and fish get caught in them

b) people keep trying to give her one; forgets to bring one with her

3a) people look bored or miserable; especially on public transport

b) a colleague thought he was flirting

4a) has always been bad at it, and wants to use jokes to build relationships

b) has problem with timing in jokes; embarrassing moment when he told boss a joke – he didn't think it was funny

5A and B

1 records   2 increased   3 exports
4 permit   5 decrease   6 appeal
7 sponsors   8 present   9 produced
10 project   11 imports   12 suspect

2.2

1B

break into a property, pretend they are someone else, win the trust of a stranger

C

a) 4   b) 3   c) 2   d) 6   e) 5

D

1 is no substitute for
2 a crash course   3 would-be
4 plausible   5 go grey
6 go undercover   7 blend in
8 confide in

2

1 speed   2 accountable   3 deterrent
4 invasion   5 law-abiding
6 recognition   7 log   8 monitors
9 microchip   10 keep track

3A

1 be painted   2 was invented, were thrown   3 has been invaded
4 is gradually being damaged/
is being gradually damaged/
has gradually been damaged/
has been gradually damaged

5 being kissed   6 to be killed
7 be found
8 had already been explored

B

2, 7

4

1 are being taught   2 are sent
3 be used   4 decide
5 will be used   6 will allow
7 be altered   8 will also send
9 was tested   10 be introduced

5A

1 I am writing with regard to

2 I have already pursued this matter

3 In order to resolve this matter

4 Please contact me within ten days

5 to confirm that this step has been taken

6 Thank you for your prompt attention to this matter

7 Yours faithfully

8 Enc: hotel receipt

2.3

1A

1 I'm ~~not~~ in favour of that

2 The way ~~what~~ I see it

3 you've got a ~~the~~ point there

4 It seems ~~that~~ to me

5 I'm agree to some extent

6 I ~~can~~ suppose so

7 ~~Is~~ fair enough but

8 I see your point ~~is~~, but

9 I'm still not ~~being~~ convinced

10 I ~~don't~~ disagree

2

1 According to the latest research, profiles on social networking sites are accurate descriptions of people's personalities.

2 Toys like dolls, electric train sets and Lego are still enjoyed by kids.

3 In many countries, for instance Japan, fish is an important part of the diet.

4 Apparently, people are attracted to partners who look like them.

5 It's been shown that coffee increases short-term memory.

6 'Soft' subjects such as Media Studies, Sports Studies and Dance are no longer being offered in some colleges.

7 Take the case of twins separated at birth who lived identical lives.

8 It's a well-known fact that children under five who watch too much television lack basic communication skills.

3A

1 illegal 2 sensible 3 unethical
4 justifiable 5 inevitable 6 disturbing
7 outrageous 8 inoffensive

B

1 sensible 2/3/4 illegal, disturbing, outrageous 5 inoffensive
6 unethical 7 inevitable 8 justifiable

REVIEW AND CHECK 1

1

1 has wanted 2 moved 3 passed
4 've/have been trying
5 've/have finally done 6 've/have told
7 's/has become 8 's/has been
9 've/have been hoping 10 added
11 has spent 12 's/has passed

2

1 b, a 2 a, b 3 b, a 4 b, a 5 a, b
6 b, a

3

1a) pulls her weight   b) is particular
2a) embarrassed   b) awkward
3a) relieved   b) satisfied
4a) two-for-one   b) non-refundable
5a) keep track of   b) monitor
6a) deterrent   b) invasion
7a) illegal   b) unethical
8a) outrageous   b) disturbing
9a) sensible   b) justifiable

4A

1 drought 2 famine 3 obesity
4 microchip 5 drug abuse

5

1 were asked 2 completed
3 scored 4 is/was thought
5 are filmed 6 are asked
7 have caused 8 be predicted
9 will face/are going to face
10 has been/was/is designed
11 were found 12 has been given

6

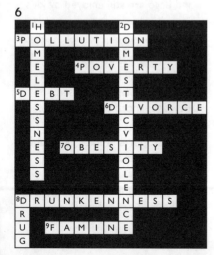

B

1 pollution 2 poverty 3 drought
4 homelessness 5 drunkenness
6 domestic violence 7 divorce 8 debt
9 drug abuse 10 obesity 11 famine

7

1 I take your point but
2 I'm in favour of that
3 I don't agree with you
4 I agree to some extent but
5 I'm still not convinced
6 You've got a point there but
7 I know what you mean but
8 I'm not so sure

8

1 anxiety 2 nervousness/nerves
3 frustration 4 disappointed
5 embarrassing 6 awkwardness
7 exhausting 8 satisfying 9 similar
10 generosity

9

1 Can you tell me what you were like ten years ago?
2 I'd be interested to know how you think you've changed.
3 Would you mind telling me what you have done that you are most proud of?
4 I wonder if/whether it's possible for a person to stay the same all his life.
5 Could you tell me who has influenced you the most?
6 I was wondering if/whether you would like to direct a movie yourself.

10A

1 help 2 was wondering, wonder
3 booking 4 Would you mind
5 Can you, Could you 6 appreciate it, be grateful

B

a) 5 b) 3 c) 6 d) 4 e) 1 f) 2

11A

1 appealing 2 sponsors 3 project
4 research 5 decrease 6 desert
7 recorded 8 permit 9 imports
10 increased

C

1 appealing 2 sponsors 3 project
4 research 5 decrease 6 desert
7 recorded 8 permit 9 imports
10 increased

TEST

1 b 2 a 3 c 4 a 5 a 6 b 7 a
8 c 9 a 10 b 11 b 12 c 13 c
14 a 15 c 16 b 17 b 18 b 19 a
20 c 21 a 22 b 23 b 24 a 25 a
26 c 27 c 28 a 29 c 30 b

UNIT 3

3.1

1A

forgetting to eat, very bad headaches, sleep problems, dry or aching eyes

B

forgetting to eat	3
ignoring friends and family	1, 4
anxiety	1
lying about time spent doing it	3
very bad headaches	4
always thinking about doing it	2
sleep problems	2
problems with school or work	3, 5
dry or aching eyes	1
not taking proper breaks	4, 5

C

1 I actually found it quite strange talking to them face to face because I'm much more used to interacting with people online.
2 It's the quizzes and other applications that get me, like there's always a new questionnaire or test for something.
3 I would often skip lunch so that I could carry on chatting.
4 To be fair, she probably asked me in person first but I suppose I'd got so absorbed in the site that I didn't hear her.
5 When a chat message came in, I couldn't resist, I'd stop what I was doing and join the conversation.

2A

1 get on with 2 criticise 3 put off
4 pay attention to 5 stubborn
6 compliment 7 take care 8 give in
9 ignore 10 neglect

B

1 took care 2 neglected 3 ignored
4 paid attention to 5 put it off
6 got on with 7 complimented
8 criticised 9 stubborn 10 gave in

3

1 not, 'm used to being
2 used to, used to
3 get used to, used to
4 take, stay
5 get used to, aren't used to
6 used to, 've got used to
7 would, used to
8 wearing, use

4

1 I used to <u>love</u> it.
2 I didn't use to <u>discuss</u> it.

3 We'd always <u>eat</u> together.

4 We'd always <u>argue</u>.

5 He's not <u>used</u> to it yet.

6 I'm getting <u>used</u> to it.

7 She can't get <u>used</u> to it.

8 I've got <u>used</u> to it.

5

1 get used to

2 used to live

3 would put/used to put/was used to putting

4 used to think

5 have got used to/am used to

6 are used to having/used to have

7 get used to sleeping

8 would get up/used to get up

9 get used to waking up

10 am used to living/used to live

11 would wash up/used to wash up

12 get used to

6A

Negative side: 2, 3

Positive side: 4

B

a) To start with,

b) For instance,/For example,

c) In addition to this,/Furthermore,

d) For instance,/For example,

e) as another example,

f) At the same time,

g) For instance,/For example,

h) To sum up,

3.2

1A

a) 3 b) 2 c) 1 d) 5 e) 4

B

1 F: even sceptics have had to regard space tourism as an area with real commercial potential

2 T: which included a week-long stay on the International Space Station

3 F: suborbital flights; space tourists experience a few minutes of weightlessness and a view of the stars before heading back to earth and gliding in for a landing

4 NG: this isn't mentioned as the writer's opinion anywhere

5 T: to develop space hotels that can offer more luxurious surroundings than the International Space Station, which was designed for research purposes, not for tourists

6 NG: we know the Space Island Group's hotel rotates, but we don't know about The Galactic Suite space hotel

7 T: Space enthusiasts are optimistic ... and expect prices to keep coming down as competition gets more vicious

8 F: there's always the prospect, however unlikely, of getting a job in one of the space hotels

C

1 the stuff of 2 sceptics

3 got on the case 4 sub-orbital

5 come up with 6 targeting

7 the going price 8 vicious

2

1 might/may take

2 will she do/is she going to do

3 's thinking of travelling

4 correct

5 'll postpone

6 'll phone and ask

7 leave

8 correct

9 are we going to eat/are we eating/will we eat

10 arrive

3

1 It's likely to be hot tomorrow.

2 Chris is hoping to find a new job.

3 I want to see Ingrid before I leave.

4 They're planning to meet at 3 o'clock tomorrow.

5 Barcelona will definitely win the championship.

6 Call me as soon as you finish.

7 She may well get her work permit tomorrow.

8 I probably won't see you tomorrow.

4A

1 Peninsula 2 remote 3 unspoilt

4 as the crow flies

5 densely populated

6 half-way between 7 edge

8 slopes 9 summit

10 off the (south-west) coast

11 close proximity

B

1 The peninsula is in close proximity to the Atlantic.

2 The Blasket Islands (off the south-west coast).

3 The Dingle Peninsula

4 Castlegregory, located on the north coast, half-way between Tralee and Dingle

5

3.3

1A

1 way 2 object 3 the first thing

4 basically 5 the point 6 what usually happens 7 key thing 8 after

2

3

1 roll 2 stir 3 unplugged

4 deal (them) out 5 pressed 6 jam

7 lean 8 sieved 9 Double-click

10 sprinkle

4A and C

1 Look up the idiom <u>where</u>?

2 I should see <u>who</u>?

3 You last spoke to her <u>when</u>?

4 I can use a question word to <u>do what</u>?

5 <u>Who's</u> waiting backstage?

6 The rain's doing <u>what</u>?

7 I'll find you <u>where</u>?

8 The <u>what's</u> too high?

UNIT 4

4.1

1A

1 was fishing, saw

2 was teaching, became

3 'd known, read

4 noticed, had left

5 had been searching, was beginning

6 had been looking, heard

7 were, 'd been walking

8 'd driven, had taken

B

1 F 2 B 3 D 4 D 5 F 6 B

7 F 8 D

2

1 had been snowing

2 had the victim been coming

3 'd/had broken

4 had you made

5 'd/had been singing

6 Had she ever done

7 hadn't been planning

8 had been making

3A

1 had been feeling/had felt

2 seemed/had seemed

3 was explaining   4 realised

5 had climbed   6 was sitting

7 had also failed/also failed

8 had begun/was beginning

9 overheard   10 rushed   11 changed

12 had used/had been using

13 told   14 brought

B

1 had been feeling

2 seemed

3 was explaining

4 realised

5 had climbed

6 was sitting

7 had also failed

8 was beginning

9 overheard

10 rushed

11 changed

12 had been using

13 told

14 brought

4A

1b 2f 3a 4d 5c 6g 7e

B

1 Computer games often use a plot of 'the quest'.

2 *Superman* is a 'rags to riches' plot.

3 *Romeo and Juliet* is an example of a 'tragedy'.

4 Detective stories are a type of 'overcoming the monster' story.

5 Humour is an element usually found in 'comedy'.

6 *Lost* is a TV series which is a 'voyage and return' story – the characters become lost when their plane crashes on a desert island.

7 Losing money can happen in the first part of a 'rebirth' story.

5

1 where there's life there's hope

2 let's cross that bridge when we come to it

3 'nothing ventured, nothing gained'

4 every cloud has a silver lining

5 what goes around comes around

6 when in Rome, do as the Romans do

7 Once bitten, twice shy

8 where there's smoke, there's fire

6A

2

B

1 stupidly   2 naturally   3 immediately
4 loudly   5 eventually/finally
6 fortunately   7 eventually/finally
8 completely

C

Sample answer

There was a thirsty crow who found a water pot and **naturally** wanted to drink from it, but the water was at the bottom of the pot and the crow couldn't reach it. At first, he just stared at the pot **dejectedly**, trying to think of what to do. **Finally**, he thought of a clever plan: he would drop small stones into the pot one by one. **Eventually** the water rose to the top, and the crow could drink it. And the moral of the story is 'Necessity is the mother of invention'.

4.2

1A

1 'd/had worked   2 'd/had saved
3 hadn't begun   4 'd/had paid
5 n't have got married
6 n't have left   7 'd/had learnt
8 have travelled

2A

1 I'd had   2 you'd   3 it would stop
4 shouldn't have   5 should have
6 shouldn't have

3

1 would stop asking her

2 I were/was at home

3 only we didn't/did not owe

4 have been told

5 you didn't/did not interrupt me/ you wouldn't/would not interrupt me

6 wish I'd/I had thought

7 shouldn't/should not have lost

8 I could see something

9 only we had/we'd more

10 should have listened

4

1 pity   2 second thoughts
3 kick themselves   4 hindsight
5 missed opportunity   6 gutted

5A

1 Janine is deaf; Dean is blind

2 Janine: by using different strategies such as watching others' breathing, feeling vibrations from the music, asking other performers to signal to her; Dean: by using the sounds he hears to understand what is happening

B

1 J   2 D   3 J   4 D   5 J   6 J   7 D
8 D

C

1 closely guarded   2 profoundly
3 develop   4 reveal
5 comprehensive   6 heightened

6A

1 up   2 up   3 to   4 on/off   5 down
6 off   7 on   8 on   9 down   10 over

B

an underwater cameraman

4.3

1

2A

1 Well, I'm not a big fan of travel books.

2 I'm not that keen on all the description.

3 Yes, what he loves about it is that they do a lot of sport.

4 Oh, yeah. He's really into football at the moment.

5 I can't stand it when the meat isn't cooked properly.

6 And the other thing I hate about them is the mosquitoes.

B

1 Well, I'm not a big <u>fan</u> of <u>travel books</u>.

2 I'm not <u>that</u> <u>keen</u> on all the <u>description</u>.

3 <u>Yes</u>, what he <u>loves</u> about it is that they do a lot of <u>sport</u>.

4 Oh, yeah. He's really into football at the moment.

5 I can't stand it when the meat isn't cooked properly.

6 And the other thing I hate about them is the mosquitoes.

3

1 was kicked out   2 is kicked out
3 worked   4 earns   5 met
6 was having   7 was waiting
8 fell   9 meets   10 delivers
11 has died   12 fall

REVIEW AND CHECK 2

1

1 thought   2 'd/had been studying
3 were coming   4 were looking
5 had rained/had been raining
6 swam   7 were sharing   8 began
9 told   10 was going   11 realised
12 was going   13 had realised
14 was shaking   15 massaged
16 'd/had recovered

2

1	a) ignored	b) neglected
2	a) complimented	b) paid attention
3	a) take care	b) get on
4	a) stubborn	b) selfish
5	a) second thoughts	b) hindsight
6	a) gutted	b) kicked
7	a) take to	b) take up
8	a) taken on	b) set up
9	a) in close proximity	b) on the edge

3A

1 proximity   2 criticise   3 cloud
4 generous   5 pity   6 forested

4

1 Are (you) thinking   2 is likely
3 will use   4 will become
5 will break   6 won't keep
7 're/are going to lose/will lose
8 starts   9 're/are meeting
10 takes off/is taking off
11 plan/'m planning
12 'll ask/'m going to ask

5

luggages   contents   outskirts
means   transports   informations
accommodations   facilyies
electricitiesy   remains   views
sceneriesy   locals   whereabouts

6

1 No, I'm used to it.

2 Yes. From the age of four I would dress up and sing for my parents.

3 That's right, but they weren't used to having children around ...

---

4 I wasn't used to sitting still for so long.

5 Yes, eventually I got used to the routine and I worked hard.

6 No, I didn't use to enjoy the music classes ...

7 He used to work for a music publisher ...

8 Yes, I still can't get used to it.

7

1 The first thing you do is to make sure

2 A key point is to make sure

3 Next

4 The key thing is to ensure

5 after you've cooked

6 The main thing is to keep

7 Basically, the object is to keep

8 After that

9 The way it works is that

10 What happens next is

8

1 I'm really keen on chillies. They're great for flavouring boring dishes.

2 I hate steak when it's rare – what I really don't like is the colour.

3 What I like about olives is their salty taste, particularly on pizzas.

4 I absolutely can't stand snails. The thought of them makes me feel sick.

5 I'm really into pasta, mainly because it's so quick to make.

6 I'm not a big fan of cheese. It's something about the smell.

7 Cherries are my favourite fruit – the thing I love about them is their taste.

8 I'm not that keen on chocolate as it's often too sweet for me.

9

1 I shouldn't have posted

2 I really wish I hadn't

3 I should have chosen

4 I shouldn't have

5 Now I wish I'd/had deleted

6 If only I were/was as slim as then and had

7 I wish he would phone and yell at me

8 If only I'd/had replied

TEST

1 a   2 b   3 c   4 a   5 a   6 c   7 a
8 b   9 a   10 b   11 c   12 b   13 a
14 b   15 c   16 a   17 b   18 c   19 c
20 b   21 c   22 b   23 a   24 b   25 b
26 a   27 c   28 a   29 b   30 a

UNIT 5

5.1

1A

1 C   2 A   3 B   4 D

B

1 tip   2 three or more   3 teenagers
4 perfumes   5 dogs, cats

C

1 c   2 b   3 a   4 b

2

1 a   2 –   3 the   4 An   5 a   6 the
7 the   8 the   9 –   10 –   11 a   12 –
13 an   14 the   15 the

3

- Remember the saying 'necessity is the mother of the invention.' When the people need the things, sooner or later someone will come up with an idea to meet that need. It could be you!

- Watch people and notice their habits. How do they do the everyday activities, such as answering the phone, handling the money or the credit cards, eating and drinking? Is there a way that one of the activities could be made easier?

- When you have an idea, write it down. Draw a picture. Give it a name. This will help your mind work on the idea further.

- Don't talk to the negative people about your ideas. The motivation is important for the creativity, and negative people can kill it.

- Talk to a friend about your ideas. Some of the most successful ideas emerge through the talking.

4A

Crossword:
1 detrimental
2 beneficial
3 revolutionise
4 enhance
5 distort
6 transform
7 damage
8 alter
(down: crown/crunch – c, h, n)

B

Oo	oO
damage alter	enhance distort transform
ooOo	ooOoo
detrimental beneficial	revolutionise

5

1 side 2 come 3 through 4 off
5 out 6 back 7 look 8 down

5.2

1B

1 Love 2 Discover 3 Health
4 Safety 5 Results 6 Cheap
7 Client 8 Deal 9 Best 10 Quality

2

1 go to great lengths
2 armchair explorers
3 dig deeper into their pockets
4 a big no-no
5 at the forefront
6 made (consumers) numb to

3

1 unless we have/get
2 closed later
3 Supposing we pay/paid
4 as long as we are/we're
5 were to accept
6 got back together
7 didn't enjoy skiing
8 Might you regret it

4

1 doesn't have, might/could get
2 were/was, would (you) say
3 have been accepted/are accepted/will
   be accepted, achieve
4 weren't/wasn't, wouldn't wear
5 will close/are going to close, comes
   forward
6 doesn't know, should tell
7 weren't/wasn't sitting, 'd/would be
8 'll/will buy, pass

5

6A

a) is far less important for
b) show an interesting contrast to
c) place greater importance on
d) there is almost no difference in
e) affects both groups more or less
   equally
f) there are significant differences in
g) only shows/shows only a slight
   variation

B

1e 2d 3g 4f 5c 6b 7a

5.3

1B

The speakers choose fines or prizes.

C

1 What do you think about simply
   ~~write~~ writing
2 How ~~much~~ do you feel about a
   fine system?
3 ~~I~~ suppose we try
4 It doesn't grab ~~for~~ me.
5 Would you consider ~~about~~ having
6 I think we're ~~running~~ on the wrong
   track here.
7 How does giving a prize for using
   only English strike you ~~out~~?
8 I'd go ~~agree~~ for that.
9 It'd be great if we ~~should~~ could get
10 I'm torn ~~up~~ between punishment
   and reward systems.
11 Could we go ~~in~~ for both?
12 let's go ~~out~~ with that.

2A

1 With **respect**, we need to be more
   focussed.
2 To be **honest**, I thought your first
   suggestion was better.
3 To put it **bluntly**, that's the worst
   idea I've heard today.
4 **Actually**, I don't think that's a very
   practical idea.
5 **Frankly**, it's just not going to work.
6 **As a matter of fact**, that's probably
   the only solution.

3A

1 obscure 2 predictable 3 absurd
4 ambitious 5 weird 6 dreadful
7 unrealistic 8 brilliant

B

1 oO 2 oOoo 3 oO 4 oOo
5 O 6 Oo 7 ooOo 8 Oo

UNIT 6

6.1

1A

1 **Act your age!**
2 I'm continually surprised by her
   maturity.
3 Yes, he looks very young **for his
   age**.
4 We're visiting an **elderly** aunt of
   Simon's.
5 Careful – that could be seen as age
   discrimination.
6 Yes, she's definitely in her **prime**.
7 I agree – they've certainly **come** of
   age now.
8 Yeah, he's so **immature**.

B

positive: 2, 3, 6, 7
negative: 1, 5, 8
neutral: 4

2

1 couldn't 2 had to 3 needed
4 obliged to 5 are able 6 managed to
7 can 8 are supposed to
9 made 10 being able to
11 wasn't allowed 12 don't have to

3

1 doesn't have to provide
2 can't make kids eat
3 didn't manage to 4 let him go
5 won't be able to
6 aren't supposed to be

4B

Speaker 1: 5 Speaker 2: 7
Speaker 3: 3 Speaker 4: 1

C

1 any age
2 having enough time to practise,
   motivation, trying out different
   instruments before choosing
3 50–69
4 maturity and energy
5 So you don't create an unhealthy
   environment for the child.
6 too soon/young
7 When the person has a particular
   vocation (for example a doctor or
   an engineer).
8 Try out lots of things to see what
   you enjoy and develop general
   skills.

D

1 c 2 e 3 b 4 d 5 a

5A

1 achievement 2 involved
3 appreciation 4 practise
5 encourage 6 judged 7 preference
8 satisfying 9 interfering 10 advice

5B

/ɪ/ little: enjoy, pretence, prefer,
   encourage
/iː/ eat: appreciate, achievement
/aɪ/ sky: oblige, advise
/e/ red: preference

6.2

1A

clothes, relationships, newspapers, (social networking is referred to indirectly: the LifeSaver programme sends video and audio from your day out to people who have signed up to receive them)

B

1 f 2 e 3 a 4 d 5 b

C

1 F 2 F 3 NG 4 T 5 T 6 NG
7 T 8 F

2

1 will have started 2 won't be using
3 'll be attending 4 need
5 will be signing 6 will involve
7 will consist 8 will have happened

3A

1 The world will be experiencing a mini ice-age at that time.
2 The average weight of an adult male will have gone down to seventy kilos.
3 Smoking will have been banned completely in all public areas.
4 Every city will own a big computer.
5 Everyone will be driving flying cars.
6 Men and women will be wearing the same clothes.
7 Poverty and famine will have halved.
8 Every company will belong to its workers.

4

1 gloomy 2 ups and downs
3 promising 4 mixed feelings
5 look on the bright 6 forward
7 upbeat 8 dread 9 despair
10 with optimism

5A

1 because 2 so as not to 3 for
4 in order to 5 so that 6 not to

B

a) 2, 6
b) 3, 4
c) 1, 5

6.3

1A

1 credit card 2 staying, alone
3 ridden, scooter 4 wear 5 late, stay 6 run, business 7 owned
8 social networking 9 part-time
10 travelling solo 11 babysit
12 pierced

2A

1

Isn't ~~that~~ it time that they banned 'size zero' models?

~~Don't~~ Doesn't it matter to you that young girls think it's normal to be so skinny?

~~It's not~~ Clearly it's not right.

2

~~Aren't you thinking~~ Don't you think that they should use technology in football games?

~~No one can't~~ Anyone can see it would be fairer.

Yeah, but surely it's more important that decisions are correct.

B

1

<u>Look</u> at this <u>picture</u>. Isn't it <u>time</u> that they <u>banned</u> 'size <u>zero</u>' <u>models</u>?

<u>Doesn't</u> it <u>matter</u> to you that <u>young girls</u> think it's <u>normal</u> to be so <u>skinny</u>?

Well you <u>should</u>. <u>Clearly</u> it's not <u>right</u>.

2

Don't you <u>think</u> that they should use <u>technology</u> in <u>football</u> games?

<u>Yeah</u>, to make <u>decisions</u>. <u>Anyone</u> can <u>see</u> it would be <u>fairer</u>.

Yeah, but <u>surely</u> it's more <u>important</u> that <u>decisions</u> are <u>correct</u>.

3A

1

So what you're saying is that

So in other words I look fat!

2

What you're getting at is

So I gather your point is that

So if I've got it right,

REVIEW AND CHECK 3

1

1 will have doubled 2 will be paying
3 will not/won't have saved
4 will be facing 5 will be discussing
6 will be living 7 will be driving
8 will have 9 will have replaced
10 will be working

2

If you want to win at sports, choose a red shirt. Research by two scientists from the University of Durham shows that a team's chance of winning is influenced by the colour of their shirts. As part of their investigation, the scientists examined football results since the end of the Second World War and found a clear connection between wearing red and winning. Teams who wore an orange or yellow shirt had the worst records.

3

1 a) promote   b) influence
2 a) commercials   b) campaigns
3 a) distorted   b) damaged
4 a) enhance   b) have a beneficial effect
5 a) elderly   b) mature
6 a) act his age   b) come of age
7 a) obscure   b) unrealistic
8 a) weird   b) dreadful

4A

1 advertise 2 achieve 3 ambitious
4 wear 5 appreciate 6 reaction

5

1 for 2 What 3 thinking 4 would
5 consider 6 different 7 get
8 strike 9 track 10 feel 11 grab
12 original 13 torn 14 go

6

1 I've got/I have mixed feelings about it.
2 taking one step forward and two steps back
3 has their ups and downs
4 I'm dreading
5 looks forward to taking exams
6 Look on the bright side.

7A

1 breakthrough 2 outlook
3 drawback/downside
4 breakdown 5 outcome
6 downside/drawback 7 checkout
8 trade-off

B

1 fire 2 newspapers
3 e-readers/e-books
4 divorce or separation
5 an election 6 having a dog
7 credit or debit cards 8 cars, motorcycles or scooters

8

1 were able to/managed to
2 couldn't/weren't able to
3 able to 4 ought not/oughtn't
5 won't be able
6 allow you to/let you
7 have to, should 8 supposed to
9 allowed to 10 make

9

1 owned 2 wanted 3 were 4 call
5 will 6 is 7 wouldn't 8 buy
9 provided 10 can 11 Unless 12 If

10A

E	N	C	O	U	R	A	G	E
Z	I	I	A	P	S	D	H	H
X	N	N	P	R	E	V	M	E
I	T	V	P	E	B	I	C	V
M	E	O	R	F	K	S	I	Z
P	R	L	E	E	V	E	K	S
R	F	V	C	R	S	S	F	V
E	E	E	I	J	U	D	G	E
S	R	S	A	T	I	S	F	Y
S	E	M	T	R	E	A	C	T
H	B	Z	E	N	J	W	H	H

B

1 appreciation   2 impressions
3 advice   4 satisfaction   5 reaction
6 encouragement   7 interference
8 preference

11

1 don't   2 Surely   3 Shouldn't
4 clearly   5 isn't   6 wouldn't

TEST

1 c)   2 a)   3 c)   4 c)   5 b)   6 a)
7 b)   8 a)   9 a)   10 c)   11 c)   12 c)
13 a)   14 b)   15 c)   16 c)   17 a)
18 b)   19 a)   20 a)   21 b)   22 b)
23 b)   24 a)   25 b)   26 a)   27 b)
28 b)   29 c)   30 c)

UNIT 7

7.1

1

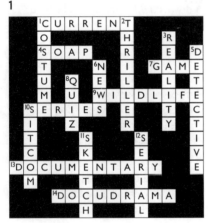

2

1 little   2 Several   3 little
4 A small number of   5 either of
6 A little   7 any   8 no

3

1 hardly any   2 quite a few   3 Both
4 a large number   5 each   6 a few
7 a large amount   8 all   9 any   10 no

4A

Speaker	Programme name	Programme type
1	*Mister Ben*	cartoon
2	*Blue Peter*	children's magazine programme
3	*Grange Hill*	soap opera for children
4	*Monty Python*	comedy sketch show

B

a) 2   b) 4   c) 1   d) 2   e) 3   f) 4
g) 1   h) 3

C

1 c)   2 e)   3 d)   4 b)   5 f)   6 a)

5A

1 back   2 up   3 down   4 out
5 across   6 out   7 into   8 out

B

1 If I say something offensive, I'm often too stubborn to take it <u>back</u>.

2 I can put <u>up</u> with a noisy hotel room more than a dirty one.

3 If someone's car breaks <u>down</u>, I know how to fix it.

4 Hard work brings <u>out</u> the best in me.

5 I come <u>across</u> as being more sociable than I really am.

6 If it turned <u>out</u> that my partner had lied to me, I would be disappointed in him.

7 If I locked my keys in my car, I would simply break <u>into</u> it.

8 When I agree to do something, I never pull <u>out</u> even if I feel ill.

C

1 broken down   2 brought out
3 pull/pulling out   4 take, back
5 put, up   6 came across   7 turn out
8 break into

7.2

1A

a newspaper

a telephone company

a travel agency

an electronics shop

B

1 e)   2 b)   3 c)   4 a)   5 d)

2

1 had taken   2 didn't remember
3 had had   4 had
5 was breaking down   6 wanted
7 wouldn't   8 had to

3

1 why I'd/had come/gone there that day

2 I'd been trying to see him since the day before

3 me to close the door and have a seat/if I could close the door and have a seat

4 how he could help me

5 him (that) I had information that Mario the Snitch would be killed the next/following day

6 what made me think this might happen

7 not to waste time asking me questions

8 (me) if/whether he should let the cops know

4A

1 to take part   2 to walk out
3 making   4 of lying
5 for doing   6 doing   a) to say
b) on changing   c) doing/having done
d) to take on   e) to pay   f) to be

B

1 e)   2 d)   3 b)   4 f)   5 a)   6 c)

5A

1 ✗   2 ✓   3 ✗   4 ✓   5 ✓   6 ✗

B

1 Although most internet writers are amateurs, many give objective information.

2 While the internet is a convenient source of information, its accessibility can also mean that this information is not trustworthy.

3 Of course there's some inaccurate content. However, it's the reader's responsibility to identify the reliable information.

4 Despite the fact that wiki contributors try to give accurate information, too many don't use reliable sources. OR Despite wiki contributors trying to give …

5 Although many amateur news websites look serious, that doesn't make them accurate.

6 While these weaknesses exist, there are reasons to trust much internet content as well.

7.3

1A

1 supplement   2 circulation
3 readership   4 broadsheet
5 sensationalism   6 columnists
7 biased   8 editorial   9 feature
10 tabloid

B

1 readership   2 sensationalism
3 broadsheet   4 supplement
5 tabloid   6 feature   7 biased
8 editorial   9 columnists
10 circulation

2

1 He's the one who's always complaining, not me.

2 You were the one who was asking about the price.

3 The incredible thing about the photo is the light.

4 The remarkable thing is that people want to buy this paper.

5 They're the ones who want to have a big party, not us.

6 The ridiculous thing is the number of adverts.

3A

1 This is totally ridiculous

2 The annoying thing is that

3 it does make me so mad when

4 you're the one who's always telling me to

5 There's no way I'd leave

6 There's no need to get into such a state

7 where on earth did I last have them

B

A: This is totally <u>ridiculous</u>. Where are my <u>keys</u>? The <u>annoying</u> thing is that I had them a <u>minute</u> ago. Oh, it <u>does</u> make me <u>so</u> mad when I can't <u>find</u> them!

B: Well, <u>you're</u> the one who's always <u>telling</u> me to put them somewhere safe. Have you tried the <u>door</u>?

A: There's <u>no way</u> I'd leave them <u>there</u>!

B: Okay, I'm just trying to <u>help</u>. There's no need to get into such a <u>state</u>!

A: I'm <u>not</u> 'in a <u>state</u>'. Now where on <u>earth</u> did I last have them?

4A

1 I reckon it's a Siamese fish

2 Surely it's a hoax photo/photo hoax

3 Perhaps there's a nuclear plant upstream

4 It might be two fish

5 I'd imagine it's genuine but it's hard to say/It's hard to say but I'd imagine it's genuine

B

a) 5   b) 1   c) 3   d) 4   e) 2

UNIT 8

8.1

1A

In the picture, the man is phoning from home; in the article, he phones from a payphone.

In the picture, the man is saving a boy; in the article, he saves another man.

1

1 hadn't walked/hadn't been walking, wouldn't have seen

2 would/might/could have been traced, had/'d phoned

3 hadn't come forward, might never have found/(never) would (never) have found

4 would/might have kept, hadn't spoken

5 would be, had/'d kept

6 wouldn't have fallen, hadn't collapsed

7 had stopped, wouldn't have leapt

8 would be, hadn't jumped

9 hadn't been, would have been killed

10 had had, wouldn't have jumped

2

1 would have asked him

2 wouldn't be sick/wouldn't have got/become/been sick/wouldn't feel/be feeling sick (now)

3 might have won (the race)

4 could he have been

5 you wouldn't/would not be living

6 if you had/'d been paying

7 be lost if Angie had

8 would you have done

3A

1 What would you have done?

2 I wouldn't have done that.

3 If I'd known when you were coming, I would've met you at the station.

B

                   /əv/
1 What would <u>you</u> have <u>done</u>?
         /əv/
2 I <u>wouldn't</u> have done <u>that</u>.

3 If I'd <u>known</u> when you were
           /əv/
<u>coming</u> I would've <u>met</u> you at the <u>station</u>.

4A and B

The experiment was about how visual images affect people's behaviour in terms of honesty.

C

1 are being watched

2 are unobserved   3 an experiment

4 psychology   5 belief

6 an honesty box   7 changed/alternated the image   8 more honest

9 three times

D

1 So that we know if we are being watched.

2 They behave less selfishly.

3 They felt surprised.

4 The poster of faces and eyes could be used for the warnings about speed cameras instead of a picture of a camera.

5 Near CCTV cameras in town centres.

5

1		C	O	M	P	A	R	E	
2	G	O	A	G	A	I	N	S	T
3	S	T	I	C	K	T	O		
4		C	O	M	E	T	O		
5				P	U	T	O	F	F
6	P	O	S	T	P	O	N	E		
7	B	E	T	R	A	Y			
				U					
8				F	O	L	L	O	W
9	A	R	R	I	V	E	A	T	
10	E	X	A	M	I	N	E		
11	W	E	I	G	H	U	P		
12	A	N	A	L	Y	S	E		
				D					

8.2

1B

A foetus   B log   C yearner
D soldier   E freefaller   F starfish

C

1 freefaller (don't like criticism)

2 foetus (shy when they first meet somebody)

3 starfish (don't like to be the centre of attention)

4 yearner (once they have taken a decision, they are unlikely ever to change it)

5 soldier (set themselves and others high standards)

6 log (easy-going, social people; freefallers are also social, but not laid back)

D

1 posture   2 (the) in-crowd
3 gullible   4 gregarious
5 thin-skinned   6 a fuss

2

1 cringe 2 bright, breezy
3 lowest ebb 4 wide awake, alert
5 sense, dread 6 despise, passion
7 sharpest 8 bounce, step 9 fussed
10 on the ball, groggy

3A

1 daydreaming 2 to solve 3 tackling
4 taking 5 clearing 6 staying up
7 to need 8 being able 9 to require
10 sleeping

B

6: Staying up all night **decreases** (not increases) the ability to hold new facts by 40%.

4

1 When I was young, my father taught me to work hard and (to) play hard.

2 Jake hates/hated not being able to play football because of his bad leg.

3 They have invited Guido to give a talk at the conference.

4 Olga has suggested going for a picnic.

5 What do you want me to do?

6 Would you mind telling us how old you are?

7 The firm didn't/doesn't expect to have to pay for the damage.

8 Can I persuade you to change your mind?

9 It isn't/It's not worth waiting any longer.

5

1 time after time 2 in the nick of time
3 to kill time 4 'm pressed for time
5 cut her holiday short
6 to make up for lost time
7 once in a blue moon
8 dragging their feet
9 for the time being
10 bided her time

6A

1 That's something 2 I'm always
3 but 4 people think
5 think much of 6 I've wasted
7 get over

8.3

1A

1 diplomatic 2 confrontational
3 sensible 4 supportive
5 collaborative 6 sensitive
7 unhelpful 8 assertive 9 focussed
10 tactful 11 aggressive 12 direct

B

positive: diplomatic, sensible, supportive, collaborative, assertive, focussed, tactful

negative: confrontational, unhelpful, aggressive

either: sensitive, direct

C

1 aggressive, confrontational
2 sensitive, supportive 3 direct
4 confrontational, aggressive
5 collaborative, sensible 6 assertive, direct 7 focussed 8 unhelpful
9 assertive 10 sensible

2A

1 Actually, there's something I've been meaning to talk to you about.

2 I don't want you to get the wrong idea, but ...

3 It's just that (often) you (often) leave your mobile on.

4 And it rings when you're not here and that's annoying./And when you're not here it rings and that's annoying.

5 Yes, but it's disturbing when people are trying to work./Yes, but when people are trying to work, it's disturbing.

6 I understand, but do you see where I'm coming from?

7 Maybe you could set it to silent when you're not here./Maybe when you're not here you could set it to silent.

8 Yes, how would you feel about that?

3

1 Actually, there's something I've <u>um</u> been meaning to talk to you about.

2 <u>Well</u>, I don't want you to get the wrong idea, but ...

3 It's just that <u>you know</u> you often leave your mobile on.

4 And it rings when you're not here and that's <u>slightly</u> annoying.

5 Yes, but it's <u>a bit</u> disturbing when people are trying to work.

6 I understand, but <u>I mean</u>, do you see where I'm coming from?

7 Maybe you could <u>just</u> set it to silent when you're not here.

8 Yes, how would you <u>er</u> feel about that?

REVIEW AND CHECK 4

1

1 would you have done things differently/would you do things differently

2 I wouldn't want/have wanted to change anything

3 If Angela and I hadn't/had not got married

4 we might/could/would/'d still be together

5 If you were to give advice/giving advice

6 what would you say

7 If I started/were starting again

8 I still think I would/'d choose

2A

1 plenty of fantastic views

2 a large ~~amount~~ number of walls

3 ~~A~~ few flats with such excellent views

4 as ~~the~~ most of the rooms are on the lower ground floor

5 close to quite a few shops and several ~~of~~ clubs

B

1 The big windows mean no privacy.

2 The flat's probably badly in need of repair.

3 The rooms are decorated in different styles (uniquely) and probably not to everyone's taste.

4 The flat's likely to be dark and damp.

5 There's likely to be too much noise.

3

1 a) serial b) series 2 a) sitcom
b) sketch show 3 a) lowest ebb
b) sharpest 4 a) groggy b) breezy
5 a) weighed up b) came to
6 a) sticking to b) analysing
7 a) sensitive b) sensible
8 a) tactful b) assertive

4A

1 promise 2 reality 3 serial
4 tabloid 5 focussed 6 aggressive

5

1 been meaning 2 hope you don't
3 the wrong 4 It's just that
5 Do you know/Do you see
6 would you feel

6

1 I'm sorry but I'll have to cut it ~~up~~ short as I'm very pressed for ~~my~~ time.

2 For the ~~present~~ time being I'm not saying anything. I'm just biding ~~on~~ my time.

3 The movie companies tend to drag their ~~two~~ feet till the last moment and then suddenly come up with the money in the ~~a~~ nick of time.

4 Time ~~and~~ after time I catch nothing and then once in a ~~the~~ blue moon I land a really big fish.

5 I had to kill ~~my~~ time because Jan was late, and we had to drive really fast to make ~~it~~ up for lost time.

7

1 told his father he wanted
2 wanted me to sing
3 hadn't given him my
4 why he didn't like
5 if/whether I had been/I'd been working/I was working
6 wouldn't be seeing Katya

8A

1 insist 2 apologise 3 promise
4 threaten 5 accuse 6 offer
7 suggest 8 admit 9 deny 10 agree

B

1 He insisted on paying for the meal.
2 I apologised for causing any embarrassment.
3 We promise to reduce taxes if you vote for us.
4 She threatened to quit the show (if she didn't get more money).
5 He accused Leona of stealing his wallet.
6 They offered to share the information (with me/us).
7 She suggested taking a break (for a few minutes).
8 He admitted stealing €5,000 from the bank.
9 He denied ever having had cosmetic surgery.
10 She agreed to make a speech.

9

1 to look 2 to be 3 expressing
4 to do 5 Recognising 6 sit
7 processing 8 watching 9 to give
10 having

10

1 take back 2 broken down
3 comes across 4 bringing out
5 pulling out of 6 put me up
7 break into 8 turned out

11

1 totally/absolutely/completely
2 is/was 3 way 4 on
5 really/absolutely 6 so 7 such
8 really 9 one
10 totally/absolutely/really/completely

TEST

1 c) 2 b) 3 b) 4 a) 5 b) 6 b)
7 a) 8 a) 9 c) 10 c) 11 c)
12 b) 13 c) 14 b) 15 a) 16 b)
17 b) 18 c) 19 a) 20 b) 21 b)
22 b) 23 a) 24 a) 25 c) 26 a)
27 b) 28 b) 29 a) 30 c)

UNIT 9

9.1

1B c

C

a) 2 b) 5 c) 1, 4 d) not mentioned
e) 3

D

1 F 2 T 3 NG 4 T 5 F 6 T
7 NG 8 T

2A

1a) to find b) studying 2a) locking
b) to lock 3a) to learn b) speaking
4a) meeting b) to do 5a) to think
b) thinking 6a) to study
b) travelling

3

1 to catch 2 chasing 3 standing
4 to be/being 5 to memorise
6 to pay 7 looking
8 picturing/to picture 9 to become
10 to say

4A

```
P I C K P O C K E T I N G I
S H O P L I F T I N G W
U A U U R U Z T K X K D J
V A N D A L I S M W D E R
T B T A X E V A S I O N Q
M R E E I T Z T R S X T N
U I R I D N N N F R R I N
G B F P T X T I Z Z T T T
G E E H A C K I N G H Y A
I R I S T A L K I N G T R
N Y T I P K C T Y B U H S
G K I D N A P P I N G E O
N V N H Q G X S X W Y F N
I M G A L C U C P V H T Z
```

B

1 arsonist 2 stalker 3 hacker
4 kidnappers 5 vandals 6 shoplifters
7 mugger 8 counterfeiter
9 pickpocket 10 tax evaders

C

Oo	arson, stalking, hacking, mugging
Ooo	vandalism, kidnapping, shoplifting, bribery
Oooo	counterfeiting, pickpocketing, tax evasion
oOooo	identity theft

9.2

1A

1 greed 2 pride 3 curiosity 4 fear
5 sympathy

B

a) 4 b) 3 c) 5 d) 1 e) 2

C

1 preys on 2 legitimate 3 plight
4 recognition 5 subtle 6 unverifiable
7 vulnerability 8 bogus

2B

a) distract b) deceive
c) pretend to be d) grab
e) switch f) be taken in

C

a) 4 b) 2 c) 1 d) 5 e) 3 f) 6

3

1 must have 2 might have
3 could have/must have

4

1 can't have got/reached/arrived/ got back
2 must have met
3 might/could have dropped/lost
4 must have come/been downloaded/been copied
5 might have/could have cut/hurt
6 can't/couldn't have seen/met

5A

February 5th – An Edinburgh man was **charged with** murder today. Police say they **suspect** 48-year-old Bill Haller of committing a series of murders but a senior police officer says they will only **accuse Haller of** one, the famous Scarsdale murder.

February 9th – A police car transporting prisoner Bill Haller crashed on the motorway today and burst into flames. Haller managed to **rescue** the driver from the burning vehicle just before it exploded. The mayor **thanked** the prisoner **for saving** the driver (who by coincidence is the mayor's son) from certain death.

February 11th – Bill Haller was **cleared of** the Scarsdale murder today as police **arrested** another suspect **for** the murder. The mayor **praised** the police **for** their detective work and **apologised** to Haller for the mistake. Haller made a statement **criticising** the police **for** their actions and **blamed** an ambitious senior police officer **for charging** him without evidence.

5B

Because he saved the mayor's son.

6A

1 Make sure you check that there are no suspicious characters nearby.
2 Be particularly careful to cover your fingers when entering your PIN.

3 Try to count the money quickly.

4 Take time to put your card away safely.

5 Never turn around if someone tries to get your attention.

6 Always be aware of people nearby.

9.3

1A

1 he reminded me ~~to~~ of that English football player

2 wait, my mind's gone blank.

3 It never ~~occupied~~ occurred to me, no.

4 before I ~~was realising~~ (had) realised what was happening, my wallet was gone

5 No, in fact it was only a minute later

6 It ~~was~~ all happened so fast

7 They seemed ~~to look~~ like students

2

1 over 2 over 3 fire 4 out
5 down 6 stuck 7 off 8 out

3A

1 C 2 F 3 D 4 B 5 A 6 E

UNIT 10

10.1

1B

a) 1, 6 b) 4, 7 c) 2, 5 d) 3

C

1b 2f 3a 4g 5e 6d 7c

D

1 shriek 2 eerie 3 corrupted
4 chattering 5 flash

2A

1 fast-paced 2 chilling 3 dull
4 moving 5 awesome 6 poignant
7 electrifying 8 brilliant 9 horrific
10 predictable 11 gripping
12 weak 13 touching 14 creepy
15 unforgettable

B

fast-paced	poignant	gripping
chilling	electrifying	weak
dull	brilliant	touching
moving	horrific	creepy
awesome	predictable	unforgettable

3A

1 that, which 2 that 3 where
4 which 5 who, that 6 whose
7 which 8 when 9 that, which
10 whose

B

1, 2, 9

4

1 A biopic is a film which tells the life story of a famous person.

2 The biopic that/which I want to review today is *Raging Bull*, which is the story of a famous boxer.

3 Robert de Niro, who plays the part of Jake La Motta, is absolutely extraordinary.

4 The film was made at a time when most biopics were of heroic figures.

5 The film, which was directed by Martin Scorsese, is now recognised as a masterpiece.

6 De Niro became interested when he read the book on which the story was based.

5A

1 highly/widely 2 harshly/ overwhelmingly/heavily
3 skilfully/sensitively 4 poignantly/ convincingly

B

1a) widely praised b) highly praised
2a) overwhelmingly criticised
b) harshly/heavily criticised
3a) skilfully directed
b) sensitively directed
4a) poignantly acted
b) convincingly acted

10.2

1A

1 A painting, not a statue, was damaged by a demolition ball.

2 The vase was broken into hundreds of pieces, not just two.

3 The painting that was damaged was broken in two. It didn't get a hole in it. It was damaged because the glue holding the frame together wasn't strong enough, not because someone put an elbow through it.

B

1 taking 2 tearing 3 shocked
4 pressed 5 walking
6 shattering 7 valued
8 embarrassed 9 employed
10 living 11 displayed 12 putting
13 being 14 used

2A

1 The people living on the other side of the river were trapped.

2 Anyone planning to go home early or wanting to take a break should let us know.

3 Walking out of the restaurant, I ran into my old boss coming in.

4 I used to work with the woman living next door.

5 I left the party quickly, not telling anyone that I was unwell.

6 Carrying a child under each arm, she ran out of the blazing building.

7 He jumped up, frightened by the loud bang, mistaking the door for a gun.

8 Walls painted white tend to attract more graffiti.

3

1 sell-out 2 alternative
3 rave reviews 4 ground-breaking
5 must-see 6 created a stir
7 mainstream 8 flop 9 hype
10 letdown

4B

1 c) 2 b) 3 a) 4 b) 5 c)

C

1 from the side 2 thirds each way, intersecting points 3 interesting
4 close 5 height, the same level

5A

1 tired 2 downs 3 don'ts
4 bounds 5 quiet 6 on 7 then
8 ready 9 cons 10 forth
11 through 12 on

10.3

1A

1 It's well worth a visit

2 Let's head over to the

3 Supposedly, they had to interrupt

4 Believe it or not, it took

5 It was originally built as

6 Well, they were founded in

7 Let's retrace our steps to

8 The story goes that he used

B

1 It's well worth a visit

2 Let's head over to the

3 Supposedly, they had to interrupt

4 Believe it or not, it took

5 It was originally built as

6 Well, they were founded in

7 Let's retrace our steps to

8 The story goes that he used

C

a) 5 b) 4 c) 3 d) 8 e) 2 f) 1

2A

1 long/length/lengthen

2 short/shortness/shorten

3 narrow/narrowness/narrow

4 wide/width/widen

5 thin/thinness/thin
6 thick/thickness/thicken
7 low/lowness/lower
8 high/height/raise/heighten*
9 large/largeness/enlarge

* When we make something higher we usually *raise* it. When feelings or effects become stronger, they are *heightened*.

B

1 narrow 2 thin 3 lowered
4 thickness, thicken
5 width, widen 6 length 7 lengthen
8 enlarge 9 high, height
10 shortened

3

1 There were just under 200 people at the party.
2 The homework should take you **roughly** an hour to do.
3 We'll be arriving at 4 o'clock or so what?.
4 The renovations cost **upwards** of one million euros.
5 We're expecting somewhere on a **in the** region of a thousand people for the conference.

REVIEW AND CHECK 5

1

1 to let 2 to turn 3 to turn, to look
4 meeting, meeting 5 talking, having
6 asking

2

1 found 2 living 3 spent 4 used
5 killed 6 arriving 7 starting
8 suffering 9 made 10 sent

3

1 a) fall for   b) deceive
2 a) taken in   b) distracted
3 a) ground-breaking b) sell-out
4 a) letdown   b) flop
5 a) Bribery   b) Tax evasion
6 a) stalkers   b) vandals
7 a) breadth   b) depth
8 a) shorten   b) lower
9 a) gripping   b) moving
10 a) knocked out   b) knocked over

4A

1 rescue 2 chilling 3 poignant
4 dull 5 hacker 6 bribery

5B

1 can't/couldn't have got
2 might/could have experienced
3 must have made

4 must have given
5 can't/couldn't have had
6 could/might have been
7 could/might have been born
8 must have been

6

1 who 2 whose 3 when 4 who
5 when/where 6 who 7 which
8 whom 9 whose 10 which

7

1 cross 2 seemed 3 so 4 much
5 like 6 reminded 7 blank 8 catch

8

1 apologised for not listening
2 blame the website for encouraging
3 be banned from showing
4 saved the plane from crashing
5 to praise children for doing/when they do
6 dreamt of being
7 is suspected of helping
8 criticising me for not helping

9

1 peace and quiet 2 ups and downs
3 pros and cons 4 give and take
5 sick and tired 6 on and on
7 now and then 8 leaps and bounds

10A and B

1 modelled 2 burnt 3 may know
4 Apparently 5 worth 6 head over
7 story goes 8 founded 9 named
10 Believe 11 retrace
12 supposedly

TEST

1 a) 2 b) 3 b) 4 c) 5 a) 6 c)
7 b) 8 a) 9 c) 10 a) 11 c)
12 b) 13 a) 14 b) 15 b) 16 c)
17 b) 18 c) 19 a) 20 c) 21 a)
22 c) 23 b) 24 c) 25 a) 26 b)
27 a) 28 c) 29 c) 30 a)

Pearson Education Limited
Edinburgh Gate
Harlow
Essex CM20 2JE
England
and Associated Companies throughout the world.

www.pearsonlongman.com

© Pearson Education Limited 2011

The rights of Frances Eales and Steve Oakes to be
identified as the authors of this Work have been asserted
by them in accordance with the Copyright, Designs and
Patents Act 1988.

First published 2011

ISBN 978-14082-5955-9

Set in Gill Sans 9.75/11.5
Printed in Slovakia by Neografia

Illustrations by KJA Artists

Acknowledgements
We are grateful to the following for permission to
reproduce copyright material:

Text
Extract Unit 4.2.5 from http://www.bbc.co.uk/radio4/
womanshour/01/2007_21_fri.shtml, BBC Radio 4
Women's Hour, By permission of Janine Roebuck;
Extract Unit 4.2.5 from http://www.guardian.co.uk/
theguardian/2007/sep/29/weekend7.weekend2#history-
byline, By permission of Janine Roebuck; Extract Unit 6.6
adapted from http://www.bbcfocusmagazine.com/features,
BBC Focus Magazine; Extract Unit 8.4 adapted from
http://news.bbc.co.uk/2/hi/health/3112170.stm,
BBC Online, bbc.co.uk/news

In some instances we have been unable to trace the owners
of copyright material, and we would appreciate any
information that would enable us to do so.

Photo acknowledgements
The publisher would like to thank the following for their
kind permission to reproduce their photographs:

(Key: b-bottom; c-centre; l-left; r-right; t-top)

Alamy Images: Ashley Cooper 28, Blend Images 61,
INSADCO Photography 41b, Kimball Hall 18, Natural
Visions 50; Corbis: Ocean 41t; Getty Images: Elie
Bernager 42, Leland Bobbe 35, Michael Blann 16; Gracey
Chirumanzu: 26r; Janine Roebuck: 26l; Kobal Collection
Ltd: PARAMOUNT 65; Reuters: Fred Prouser 20; Steve
Oakes: 68l, 68r; Linda Storey: 29, 38, 42t, 42b, 52l
(background), 52r (background); Thinkstock: Comstock /
Jupiterimages 62, Creatas Images 19, Hemera 8r, 21, 30l,
52l, iStockphoto 8l, 9l, 30r, 48, 52r, 69

All other images © Pearson Education

Picture Research by: Kay Altwegg

Every effort has been made to trace the copyright holders
and we apologise in advance for any unintentional
omissions. We would be pleased to insert the appropriate
acknowledgement in any subsequent edition of this
publication.